HE LOVED THEM TO THE END

GABRIELE CINGOLANI

# He Loved
# Them to the End

MEDITATIONS ON THE GOSPELS OF THE PASSION

Translated by Maria Domenica Iocco

ST PAULS

Alba
House

Originally published in Italian by Radio Maria, Toronto, under the title *Li amó sino alla fine: Meditazioni sui Vangeli della Passione*, © 1998 by Radio Maria Canada.

Line drawings © 1998 by Antonio Caruso.


Library of Congress Cataloging-in-Publication Data

Cingolani, Gabriele, 1940-
    [Li amó sino alla fine. English]
    He loved them to the end: meditations on the Gospels of the passion / Gabriele Cingolani; translated by Maria Domenica Iocco.
       p. cm.
    Includes bibliographical references.
    ISBN 0-8189-0903-X (alk. paper)
    1. Jesus Christ—Passion—Meditations.  I. Title.

    BT431.3.C5613 2002
    232.96—dc21

                          2001033493


Produced and designed in the United States of America by the Fathers and Brothers of the Society of St. Paul, 2187 Victory Boulevard, Staten Island, New York 10314-6603, as part of their communications apostolate.

ISBN: 0-8189-0903-X

**Printing Information:**

Current Printing - first digit   1   2   3   4   5   6   7   8   9   10

Year of Current Printing - first year shown

2002   2003   2004   2005   2006   2007   2008   2009   2010

# TABLE OF CONTENTS

## ACT III: THE TRIAL

## ACT IV: CALVARY

# Table of Contents

# INTRODUCTION

The Passion of Jesus Christ is the greatest love story of all time. It is impossible to go through life without coming into contact with it and hearing it recounted.

"God so loved the world that he gave his only Son" (Jn 3:16) who, "having loved his own who were in the world, he loved them to the end" (Jn 13:1). For God, loving to the end means to love without end. It is a love that has its origin in the Trinity and becomes human, historical, cosmic.

Since this love is made manifest in the cross, it creates problems for us. The cross makes more of an impression on us than does the love it manifests. We give more importance to the torn flesh, the flowing blood, the agony and the anguish than to love. It has been so for centuries.

In this book we dare to propose a new kind of meditation on the Passion of Jesus.

At the same time, it must be noted that the Gospels are the principal guides for our reflections. This is not because theology or popular devotion or mystical experience have no value, but because we felt it essential to channel and integrate everything along biblical lines.

Meditation on the Passion of Jesus has always supported the spiritual life of Christians, and has also produced and nurtured whole schools of spirituality. In the last decades, however, it seems to have lost some of its popularity. It has been set aside by the general crisis in traditional methods of prayer and has been replaced by newer forms of meditation centered on the Word of God. On the other hand, exegetical studies on the Passion of Jesus have greatly developed, although generally they do not lend themselves to meditation.

Thus we are faced with an age-old problem. On the one hand, those who study risk meditating insufficiently; their research illuminates the mind and appeases curiosity, but it does not warm the heart. On the other hand, those who meditate risk not studying enough. They can develop the theme well, but are in danger of straying from the Bible.

We have made an effort in these pages to reconcile both aspects. The meditative reader will judge how successful we have been.

The content of the Gospels is always in the foreground, according to the most updated exegetical research. Theological reflection, the experience of the Church, affective and emotional aspects are all accorded their own space but not free rein.

The spiritual tradition of my Passionist Family is obviously likewise present in this work, starting with our founder, St. Paul of the Cross, who is an unsurpassed master in this matter.

⁂

Here is a brief explanation of specific aspects of the procedure we have adopted.

The "Gospel of the Passion" can refer to two things: the account of the Passion in the Gospel, or the whole Gospel considered in the light of the Passion. The meditations in this book have been written with the first of these in mind.

Both in our research and in the writing, we have been continually bothered by an uncertainty, and until now we are not sure of having made the correct choice: how to present in a unified manner meditations based on four separate accounts of the Passion, each containing different messages, or at least accentuating different aspects of the same message? Each narrative includes a complex catechetical scheme. It contains an "acculturated" announcement of salvation, adapted to the recipient community.

We had to make a choice: either to offer four sets of meditations, which would have made this book burdensome and implied numerous repetitions; or to unify the meditations on the four accounts, which would have put some pressure on their individual messages.

We opted for the second alternative, trying to avoid these pressures as much as possible while stressing the characteristics peculiar to each evangelist.

We took into account the exegetical details of the specialists only when they seemed helpful in approaching the mystery. In each case our choice may be open to discussion, but we have tried to avoid the temptation of the researcher—to report everything we have discovered.

It might have been beneficial to set forth, at the beginning of each meditation, a synopsis of the corresponding Gospel passage. We omitted it, once again for the sake of brevity.

The names of the evangelists have been abbreviated also in the text: Mt for Matthew, Mk for Mark, Lk for Luke, Jn for John. The term "Synoptics" refers to the Gospels of Mt, Mk and Lk because they converge on many points. We also avoided using parentheses around biblical quotations, for visual effect.

❧

Finally, here are two suggestions on how to use this book.

**1. The Scene** is the point of the meditation. One or more may be used for any meditation. It depends on the time you have available and on the fruit that can be drawn from the subject. You must not hurry to see what follows. If you wish to do so, then use the book for spiritual reading, which is a different kind of religious experience. Should the scene not offer an inspiration for prayer or emotional involvement because it is loaded with abstract argumentation or for other reasons, please skip it and move on.

The drawings of the face of Jesus and the other illustrations are an integral part of the text. They are scenes worthy of meditation in and of themselves.

**2. The Method** is necessary to begin, but it is reduced to the minimum, according to the demand of these busy times in which we live. It consists of three simple steps, expressed by the verbs: reflect, pray, promise. These are printed only in the first meditation of every chapter, to avoid encumbering the text.

**Reflect.** This is the subject of the meditation. For purposes of recall and orientation, it contains a summary of the facts along with any exegetical and theological elements which will facilitate their comprehension in view of the spiritual fruit to be derived from the meditation. In this phase, the use of the reasoning and argumentative faculties of the memory and intellect prevail.

**Pray.** This is the most important part of the meditation. Reflection prepares us for prayer, otherwise meditation would be an exercise of the intellect alone. But praying is a most delicate and personal kind of activity. No one can pray in place of another. Therefore this section is the shortest part of the meditation. It is like giving the tone so that each may sing on his own, under the direction of the Holy Spirit. You are not to feel bound to the tone you are offered. At times, following it may lead you astray from your own personal prayer tone. You must perceive your own wavelength on which to abandon yourself to the attraction of divine love.

What prevails in this phase is the exercise of the will, emotions, heart, and adhesion to the interior attractions inspired by the Holy Spirit. We suggest that you read meditatively the material presented under the heading Reflect. Then verify whether the material under the heading Pray, which is always printed in italics, suits your style of personal prayer. If so, close the book and continue praying as long as you can.

**Promise.** It is important to end the meditation with a practical commitment, once called a resolution. The Passion of Jesus has the power to transform our lives. The goal of meditating upon the Passion is to live the Passion. In order to start this process, an effort of our will is necessary, especially at the beginning, to gradually link our lives to the Passion. What prevails in this phase is the work of the intellect and of the will for a concrete decision capable of transforming our lives.

To those who will use this instrument as nourishment of their own spiritual life, it is my desire that the Passion of Jesus might enter and always remain in their hearts.

*The Author*

# Act I

# The Last Supper

*Jesus' Passover Supper with his disciples, during which the institution of the Eucharist took place, is recounted in the New Testament with abundant and complex details. The contents of the narrative require special consideration.*

*Some scholars do not consider the Last Supper to be part of the Passion narrative. However, at the Last Supper Jesus explains the meaning of his Passion, anticipates the content of it and establishes the rite that will convey it throughout the centuries in his memory. Moreover, when the Passion narratives are used in the liturgy they always include the Supper. Christian devotion has always seen the Last Supper as an integral part of the Passion.*

*We will follow this opinion and, maintaining that the Supper is the first act of the Passion, we will begin with the scenes of its immediate preparation.*

# I. THE VISE TIGHTENS

Mt 26:1-16    Mk 14:1-11    Lk 22:1-6    Jn 11:45-53 and 12:1-8

*The evangelists introduce the story of Christ's Passion with scenes that move towards a final explosion of opposition. In Mt and Mk, two scenes of rejection frame the story of Christ's love.*

## SCENE 1: THE CONSPIRACY FORMALIZED

**Reflect.** The leaders' aversion towards Jesus, which pervades the entire Gospel, reaches a climax. The decision to eliminate Jesus has been brewing for some time. Now it is formalized. "Then the chief priests and the elders of the people gathered in the palace of the high priest, who was called Caiaphas, and took counsel together in order to arrest Jesus by stealth and kill him. But they said: 'Not during the feast, lest there be a tumult among the people,'" Mt 26:3-5.

The manner in which this will happen remains unclear, yet the action is assured. Jesus' presence has become unbearable. Eliminating him is for the common good.

Just as determined is Jesus' decision to bring to completion the work he came to do: "You know that after two days the Passover is coming, and the Son of Man will be delivered up to be crucified," Mt 26:2.

He enters into his Passion fully aware of what is to come and accepting it.

Two needs reach a climax simultaneously: one, that of love, which needs to give itself totally and unconditionally; the other, that of hatred, which needs to vent its rage to the point of destroying whatever or whoever stands in its way.

3

Indifference or the distancing of oneself from what is truly worthwhile and from love—in the end, from Christ himself—eventually leads to the destruction of all relationships.

**Pray**. *Jesus, it is already evident that the meaning of your Passion is found in the opposition between good and evil, between love and the refusal to love. How can I not take sides? Help me to always take your side.*

**Promise**. Christ's Passion must become a vital part of my own life. I promise to meditate upon it regularly.

## SCENE 2: A FRAGRANT DEATH

In Bethany, where Jesus spends the night when he visits Jerusalem, his friends invite him to share a meal. An unknown woman pours costly ointment on his head. Mt, Mk, and Jn relate this scene to the Passion, while Lk 7:36-39, places it in a different context and links it to the forgiveness of sins. In Jn and Lk the woman anoints Jesus' feet. According to Jn the ointment is worth three hundred denarii and it is poured over his feet by a friend, Mary of Bethany.

A penetrating fragrance invades the dining room, the lungs, the very breath of those present. Someone complains that it is being wasted. In Mt it is the disciples, and Mk even says they are "infuriated at her." In Jn it is Judas who protests, claiming that the perfume could have been sold to benefit the poor.

Jesus defends the woman's kind action with such powerful words that all are astounded: "Let her alone. Why do you trouble her? She has done a beautiful thing to me. For you always have the poor with you, and whenever you will, you can do good to them; but you will not always have me. She has done what she could; she has anointed my body beforehand for burying. And truly, I say to you, wherever the Gospel is preached in the whole world, what she has done will be told in memory of her," Mk 14:6-9.

The reference Jesus makes to the poor is one of the most abused phrases of the Gospel. Jesus does not mean that poverty is unavoidable in society, as if to appease the conscience of those who are not doing enough to eliminate it. He is saying that the woman has understood, through the Holy Spirit, that he is about to die, and no one is poorer than he who is close to death.

Thus, this "waste" is justified for the following reasons.

It is an expense for the poor, an expense justified especially during Passover. At this moment Jesus is the poorest of all.

It is a royal honor, because the woman anoints his head, a custom reserved for kings.

It is an act according to the law prescribing the anointing of the dead. After his death Jesus will be buried hurriedly because of the continuing Passover ceremonials. Since there wouldn't be time for the ritual anointing, the women will decide to return the next morning, but they will not find Jesus' body. The woman anticipated the anointing of Jesus' dead body.

It is an act of love, for only this woman secretly understands Jesus' innermost sentiments as he nears his final hour.

It is the Gospel, that is a sign of discipleship and witness to Jesus. That is why it will be recounted throughout the world wherever the Gospel is proclaimed.

Every time we perform an act of love—for the poor, a stranger, a family member—we proclaim the Gospel. We anoint Jesus. Those who are the recipients of our acts of love also receive the good news, a newness of life that comes from the following of Christ.

*O Jesus, may I recognize and share in the moments of solitude of those who are close to me. Inspire me with the same intuition and understanding towards others as the woman of Bethany had towards you.*

Not one of Jesus' disciples or friends really understands what Jesus is feeling now that his death is imminent. Only a stranger comprehends. Often people for whom we have little regard because they are non-Christian or non-practicing Christians behave better than the followers of Christ. We must never criticize what is good; rather, we must support and emulate it.

## Scene 3: Judas the infiltrator

We move from a scene of fellowship to one of betrayal. Mt suggests that the two scenes are taking place simultaneously: while in Bethany a woman expresses love and allegiance, in Jerusalem Judas is dealing with Jesus' adversaries, planning how he will hand him over.

"Hand over" is another expression to indicate the Passion. Jesus uses it each time he reveals what is to come, and to unfold his willingness to abandon himself to it.

The decision to do away with Jesus had been taken. Judas presents the occasion to put it into action. The evangelists specify that money is one of the motivating factors behind the betrayal. For Mt it is a matter of thirty pieces of silver, a price set by the law for a slave.

Lk and Jn signal Satan's entrance into the scene; he is the hidden orchestrator of the Passion. "Then Satan entered into Judas called Iscariot, who was of the number of the twelve," Lk 22:3.

Here he is again. After having tempted Jesus in the desert as he entered public life, Satan had distanced himself "until an opportune time," Lk 4:13. He had reappeared on diverse occasions during his ministry. This moment is the "opportune time" for him to return with all his forces against Jesus. He begins by seizing one of his disciples, a table companion who "repented" being his follower and became a spy. Betrayer is the word used in the Bible.

Jesus awaits his "hour" to hand himself over and to give his life for the salvation of the world. Judas searches for the opportune moment to hand him over.

We will come back to Judas. For the moment the evangelists introduce the actors of the drama: Jesus, the disciples, the adversaries, Judas, Satan. All are on stage and the lights are on. The story of humankind is an extension of Jesus' Passion. Each of us has a part, and we play it by either using or abusing our own freedom.

The evangelists' unanimity in citing money as a determining motive of Judas' betrayal is striking. The corruptive power of money is immeasurable. Western society confirms this today more than ever. We forget our values and our spiritual dimension for material wealth. Even Christians sell off Christ and the Gospel.

*Jesus, in my time also, the story of your Passion continues. Always help me to be on your side: love, detachment, the gift of my life in imitation and in memory of you.*

Let us not allow our possessions to possess us. Because of the traumatic nature of the Judas story we naturally see it as distant and exceptional. Yet there is an easy way to become Judas. It can slip into our attitudes and into our choices. When in our lives as Christians something is valued more than Christ, we have taken or are about to take Judas' side.

# II.  THE LAST SUPPER

Mt 26:17-35    Mk 14:12-31    Lk 22:7-38    Jn 13:1-20

*From the accounts of the Synoptic Gospels it is apparent
that Jesus' Last Supper was simultaneously the celebration of
the Hebrew Passover and the establishment of the Christian
Easter, with the institution of the Eucharist.*

*In Jn's Gospel, these two events do not appear to be
clearly linked. It may be that Jesus celebrated the Passover at
another time, however Jn does give an account of the atmosphere during the Lord's parting Supper. This grandiose and
highly expressive event is made up of a cluster of scenes to be
meditated upon one by one.*

### SCENE 1: AN OVERFLOWING HEART

**Reflect**. The Passover meal had to be prepared. A suitable
place, prescribed foods, and a family gathered together were
essential. Jesus, by commissioning two of his disciples to prepare the meal, provides for his disciples and for himself through
the courtesy of a friend who has made a room available for them
to dine in. In Lk the two disciples are Peter and John, while in
Mt they may be more than two.

In Lk it is Jesus who initiates the preparations, while in Mt
and Mk it is the disciples who remind him that the Passover must
be prepared.

Jesus is obviously in full control of the situation. While his
enemies plot against him and one of his disciples destroys the
bond of friendship between them, Jesus prepares the final stage
in his journey of love. To his anonymous benefactor he sends
this message: "My time is at hand; I will keep the Passover at
your house with my disciples," Mt 26:18.

9

In the way Jesus expressed himself, his "time"—or his "hour"—suggests many things. It can refer to his betrayal, his arrest, his death, and his glorification. But it is always associated with a sense of completion and fulfillment. It is the *kairos*, that is, the time in which God intervenes and operates in history. The principal stages are the cross, the resurrection and the final judgment. The Supper is associated with these, and for that reason it is an important time. It is also an essential crossroad for the future.

Jesus emphasizes the presence of his disciples because they are an expression of the essential rapport between himself and humanity. Lk stresses Jesus' emotional involvement as he approaches this gathering with his disciples: "With what longing I have desired to eat this Passover with you before I suffer," 22:15.

Jn does not describe the preparations for the Supper; instead he zeros in on Jesus' emotional state: "When Jesus knew that his hour had come to depart out of this world to the Father, having loved his own who were in the world, he loved them to the end," 13:1.

The events of the Supper take Jesus' love to extreme heights, to the limitless bounds of his divine love.

**Pray**. *Jesus, if this Supper is so important to you, and you want to partake of it with your disciples—with me—it must mean that I cannot do without it. In your gesture of love resides something which is essential to my existence.*

**Promise**. The Last Supper alludes to the sharing of life. God adopts this language to reveal his plan to share himself with me. My mind and heart must be open to the inexhaustible and all-embracing treasures of the Lord's Supper.

SCENE 2: THE WASHING OF THE FEET SIGNIFIES
THE GIVING OF ONE'S LIFE

Alone among the evangelists, Jn tells us that Jesus washed the apostles' feet before the Supper. This service was reserved for slaves. For Jesus it is an expression of the service love renders, even unto the giving of one's life.

In the Synoptic Gospels Jesus' love reaches its summit when he gives himself as food and drink under the species of bread and wine, signifying the gift of life. For Jn Jesus' love reaches its climax when the Son of man washes the feet of humanity, that is, purifies humanity of all sin by sacrificing himself out of love and rising from the dead.

The expressions "took off his cloak," v. 4 of chapter 13 and "put his cloak back on," v. 12, suggest the passage from death to resurrection. In fact, Jesus used the same terminology when he said: "This is why the Father loves me, because I lay down my life in order to take it up again. No one takes it from me; on the contrary, I lay it down freely. I have power to lay it down, and I have power to take it up again," Jn 10:17-18.

It is a gift freely given that cannot be repaid. It can only be accepted. Peter does not understand this, just as he will not understand the Passion. How can he accept a gift that he knows he does not deserve and which he cannot repay? Acceptance of such unconditional love requires humility. We are not worthy of the Eucharist, of salvation, yet it is a gift we cannot do without.

"Afterward you will understand," Jesus says to Peter. Jn explains this in the last chapter of his Gospel: "Afterward" means after the Passion, after the dramatic experience of his fragile state. After his restoration through forgiveness, and his declarations of unconditional love, Peter "will understand" and will be ready to follow Jesus, he, too, with the gift of his own life.

"Then you also ought to wash one another's feet," Jesus concludes. This corresponds to "do this in remembrance of me,"

11

which ends the account of the Supper in Lk and in the apostle Paul, 1 Cor 11:24-25.

In Jesus' parting discourse, Lk includes the theme of true greatness. Perhaps he is thinking about problems in the community for which he writes. He admonishes that the criteria for true greatness and authority among Christians are opposite to those of secular society. "The greatest among you shall be like the youngest, and the leader like the one who serves," 22:26. This is a teaching which is in tune with the Eucharist and the washing of the feet.

The dynamism of love is mysterious. It is inconceivable and inaccessible, yet we are asked to live it. The gift comes from Jesus, binds us to one another and returns to him. Yet it does not leave us unconnected. It engages our entire responsibility.

*O Jesus, the gentle touch of your love confounds me. It is so with each articulation of your Passion, which you anticipate in the Eucharist. Allow me to enter and remain in this mystery of love until my own life is transformed by it.*

The gesture of the washing of the feet is for Jesus another way of teaching us charity, promulgating the new commandment, and foreshadowing the gift of his life in the Eucharist. I commit myself to putting all this into practice to the best of my abilities, especially when people and situations most require it of me.

## Scene 3: The betrayer unmasked

In Mt and Mk the Supper begins with Jesus' announcement that someone will betray him. In Lk this occurs after the Eucharist and in Jn after the washing of the feet. All of the evangelists signal the fact that Jesus is aware of the situation and in control of events. Judas is convinced he is plotting secretly, protected by the darkness, but the evangelists shine a spotlight on him.

During the most intimate and tender of moments, Jesus' announcement is a heavy blow. "One of you will betray me, one who is eating with me," Mk 14:18. "Behold the hand of the one who will hand me over is with me on the table," Lk 22:21. "It is he to whom I shall give this piece of bread when I have dipped it," Jn 13:26.

An alarm sounds among the disciples. All are under accusation. Is it possible to betray another without being aware of it? "Is it I, Lord?" Mt adopts the title of the resurrected—Lord—suggesting that all Christians must continually ask this question to Christ the Lord. Only Judas uses rabbi, or master: "Is it I, Master?" This indicates that he has broken the relationship of love and fellowship with his Lord. He has lost all faith and love. Remember, Jesus had told his disciples not to use the title of rabbi, Mt 23:7-8.

The identity of the betrayer is not clearly indicated in Jesus' answer. For Jn, only the disciple whom Jesus loved is told who he is. But the betrayer is made aware that Jesus knows everything. "*You* said it," Mt 26:26. It is an uncompromising answer, which Jesus will use for the chief priest and for the Roman procurator. It means: it is your choice, your sentence.

Thus is God's judgment on individuals and on humanity. He does not condemn us because he is love, but he accepts the choices we make of our own free will. In this case, Judas has chosen to destroy Jesus, and in the process the very essence of his own being.

In the Synoptic Gospels, the mystery which pervades the Bible and troubles believers reappears: How do we reconcile God's sovereignty and foreknowledge with human freedom? "The Son of man goes as it is written of him, but woe to that man by whom the Son of man is betrayed. It would have been better for that man if he had never been born," Mt 26:24. Judas is no marionette. He freely chose to betray. Now he is fully responsible for it.

How dreadful to betray the Lord Jesus. Love, by its very

nature, cannot coerce love. Jesus' words seem to be an insurmountable barrier to the possibility of Judas' salvation, especially when we read: "None of them was lost except the son of perdition, that the Scripture might be fulfilled," Jn 17:12.

Judas remains unresponsive to love. Jesus had washed his feet; perhaps he fed him his body and blood; he revealed to him that he knows what he is about, and later on he will call him friend. It is hopeless. Love cannot enter unless we allow it to. There is no social or religious rank, even at the highest level, that can guarantee the permanence of love.

The insistence of the evangelists regarding Judas' role in the Passion seems to be merciless. We cannot tear this page from the Gospel. Judas remains an essential figure so that we can see what a misguided life is like. He is the icon of failure. He depicts the drama of the human being without God. He gets sidetracked. Anything can overtake him, even despair.

*Is it I Lord? To what measure and to what frequency does Judas live in me? Am I following you or am I betraying you? Am I looking for you or for something else? Perhaps myself?*

By meditating on Christ's Passion I keep alive those ties with him which are rooted in my baptism and nourished by the Eucharist. It gives me that daily energy I need to keep alive my promise to imitate Jesus.

## SCENE 4: THE OLD AND THE NEW PASSOVER

Lk distinguishes better than the other evangelists the two subjects of the Last Supper: the rite of the Hebrew Passover and the beginning of the Christian Easter, with the institution of the Eucharist. Lk's words in 22:15-18 do not yet refer to the Eucharist, rather to the Hebrew Passover. Having expressed his ardent desire to partake of this Passover, Jesus adds: "'I tell you I shall not eat it until it is fulfilled in the kingdom of God.' And he took a cup, and when he had given thanks he said: 'Take this and divide it among yourselves; for I tell you that from now on I shall not drink of the fruit of the vine until the kingdom of God comes.'" The cup is not yet the Eucharistic chalice, which will be consecrated in v. 20, following the consecration of the bread, v. 19. It is the last time that he will eat and drink on earth. The next time it will be completely different, in the fulfillment of the kingdom, that is, after his death and resurrection.

Jesus in effect declares that the ancient Passover ends here. As it does so, he initiates a new one, his own, which is total liberation, a definite passage to the shores of salvation with the inauguration of God's kingdom.

The Hebrew Passover unfolds in a complex ceremony composed of fourteen principal rituals, among which is the sharing of four cups of wine, each having its own special significance.

These are the fourteen rituals: first cup, washing of the hands, tasting the celery, first unleavened bread, narration of the Passover, second cup, second unleavened bread, bitter herbs, third unleavened bread, paschal lamb preceded by an hors d'oeuvre, festive continuation of the meal, third cup. Perhaps this third cup, the twelfth ritual, becomes the Eucharistic chalice. This is the moment in which the new Passover replaces the old one. The Hallel canticle follows, which consists of the psalms of praise, 114-118, and then the fourth cup concludes the meal.

In Lk Jesus' conversation has the rhythm of a final farewell as it does in Jn, although in a fuller way and in a different context. In the biblical world, as in the Greco-Roman world, there are examples of figures on the verge of departing the scene who give a speech which becomes a testament, in which they make predictions, leave instructions and entrust duties. All these elements are present in Jesus' words during the Supper. In addition, he includes his reasons for his eventual return, for carrying on and for his victory. Death will not mean defeat or the end of everything.

During the Supper Jesus is aware that he is at the center

of the plan of salvation. He is at the end of one era and at the beginning of another. He is God carrying out God's plan, and he is man, recipient of God's love.

Up to this point the Supper was a reminder of the past, from this point forward it is a foretaste of the future. Not only is it the imminent future of death and resurrection, but also the future of the end of times. In fact, the final consumption of the Supper, which he is instituting, will occur then: the banquet of the kingdom, which Jesus will share with all humanity. The new ritual will not only bring the past to the present, but will project the present into the future.

*O Jesus, the paschal meal is for you a climactic moment. It seems that your plans are already accomplished. How marvelous to simply breathe in the atmosphere which is preparing the event.*

The first fruit which comes from meditating on the Passion is that I discover its presence in the Eucharist, as sacrifice in the Mass and as permanent sacrament in the tabernacle. The fruit that follows is rediscovering it in my life and in the lives of others.

## SCENE 5: BREADS AND BREAD

In the institution of the Eucharist Jesus adopts the same gestures he used in the multiplication of the loaves. Let's trace it in Mk.

During the Supper: "He took bread, and blessed, and broke it, and gave it to them," 14:22.

During the first multiplication of the loaves: "And taking the five loaves… Jesus… blessed, and broke the loaves, and gave them to the disciples to set before the people," 6:41.

During the second multiplication of the loaves: "He took the seven loaves, and having given thanks he broke them and gave them to his disciples to set before the people," 8:6.

The gesture always includes four actions: taking, blessing or giving thanks, breaking, and distributing. Not all the evangelists list all four.

The relationship between the events is even more profound.

The first multiplication of the bread takes place on Jewish territory and twelve full baskets are left over. This is a sign that Jesus is able to nourish all twelve tribes of Israel.

The second multiplication takes place on pagan ground and seven baskets of loaves remain. This is a sign of universality and completeness and it announces that Jesus will nourish all of humanity.

But how? The answer is revealed during the Last Supper: by giving himself as nourishment. The multiplications of the loaves which preceded the Supper led to this multiplication of the Eucharist, the inexhaustible and universal nourishment of divine life.

Jesus' sermon on the bread of life, in Jn 6, which follows the multiplication of the loaves, confirms and explains this. In Mk also we understand the importance of the rapport between bread and Eucharist, in the severe rebuke addressed to the disciples for their obtuseness following the first multiplication of the loaves.

The evening after the event, Jesus goes to meet his disciples, walking on the lake. They are terrified because they think they see a ghost. Mk comments: "They did not understand about the loaves; instead, their hearts were hardened," 6:52. Why does he say this? Is this comment out of place? Just the opposite.

If they did not understand the significance of the bread, they did not understand Jesus and cannot recognize him. Walking on water or performing any other miracle is much easier than offering his life as nourishment. The loaves of bread and the Bread are both symbols of Jesus' mission of universal salvation.

Mk offers similar explanations after the second multiplication of the loaves.

In the bread of the Supper, Jesus fulfills all of the allusions contained in the multiplication of the loaves: the significance of the gathering of God's people nourished also by his word, the forgiveness of sin, and the significance of God's compassion in taking care of his people beyond all expectations and in all of his other interventions. To give food and nourishment means to give life.

Like the Passion, so the Eucharist is part of the plan Jesus had in his heart from the very beginning. It is all one.

*O Jesus, grant that I may understand always and more fully what you want to tell me and what you want to tell the world through the Eucharist.*

The Eucharist is at the center of Jesus' life and mission. His miracles and teachings tend towards this. It must also become the center of my life. To the extent it is not, I pledge to make it the focus of my life and mission.

## Scene 6: Broken bread, broken body

The accounts of the institution of the Eucharist are not identical. The slight differences are perhaps due to the community's liturgical use or to the narrator's theological perspective.

Important is the significance that Jesus wants to confer on his mission and on his imminent death: to nourish, to save and to give his life.

Jesus' life is approaching the end. His body is about to be handed over and broken. By proclaiming that the bread is his body he makes of it a sign of his death for all of humankind. This is the last announcement of the Passion, and already it contains the Passion.

The traditional rituals of the Hebrew Passover now acquire new meaning: it is no longer the crossing of the Red Sea, from slavery to national freedom, but Jesus' passage from death to life.

It is humanity's crossing from subjection to sin to friendship with God, thanks to the new nourishment.

"Take, eat it; this is my body," Mt 26:26.

"Take; this is my body," Mk 14:22.

"This is my body which is given for you. Do this in remembrance of me," Lk 22:19.

After having fed the people in different ways, Jesus now nourishes everyone in a new manner: with his body. There is nothing abstract about it, for Jesus gives himself, as Lk explains. His death is not without meaning; in fact, it is a gift that produces energy. It is nourishment which gives strength. It is "given for you."

Lk's formula is more descriptive. Perhaps it indicates that he is drawing from a liturgical tradition similar to that of the apostle Paul, 1 Cor 11:24. It also indicates that he is writing for a mature community which has moved from conversion to fellowship, which is not satisfied to live the Eucharist in a passive way but wants to live the Eucharist more fully. "Do this in remembrance of me" bonds our life to the Eucharist.

The new commandment to love one another as Jesus loved us, culminates in the giving of our lives. This new commandment is to be put into practice in memory of Christ insofar as we are his table companions. It is not a matter of simply repeating the ritual. Instead, we must express its contents anew, that is, we must bring Christ's love into our Christian lives for it was Christ who gave his life for the salvation of the world.

"In remembrance of Christ" means to imprint Christ in our lives through the power of the Eucharist. It means making the Passion a way of life individually and as communities. It means living on the Jesus-level.

*O Jesus, through the Eucharist you made your life and love available to me. You are ever present on the altar as sacrifice and sacrament, to embrace my life as it unfolds and is spent for you.*

I must be careful not to reduce my Christian practices to

nothing more than sporadic manifestations. There are Christmas and Easter Christians, funeral and pilgrimage Christians. But only by following Jesus each day and by drawing energy from the Eucharist each Sunday can we be true Christians.

## SCENE 7: THE WINE, BLOOD OF THE NEW COVENANT

Jesus' words as he distributes the bread during the Last Supper, are linked to the words pronounced over the loaves multiplied for the hungry multitudes. By using terms like "breaking" and "giving" in reference to his body he alludes to his death.

Jesus' words as he shares the cup of wine also point to his death because they bring together the concepts of "blood" and "cup." Jesus used the word "cup" on other occasions to refer to his death. When the two brothers, James and John, ask to sit with him in his kingdom he answers: "Are you able to drink the cup that I am drinking?" Mk 10:38. In the garden of Gethsemane Jesus asks his Father: "If it be possible, let this cup pass from me," Mt 26:39. That is, let the death which is imminent pass me by.

"Drink of it all of you; for this is my blood of the covenant, which will be poured out for many," Mt 26:27-28. "Many" in biblical language means a multitude or totality. Lk uses "poured out for you," 22:20.

In the Hebrew Passover meal, this cup was the third serving of wine, called the memorial cup or the cup of the blessing. The cup, decorated by a wreath of flowers, was passed around for the table companions to partake of it. It served as a reminder of God's presence among his people, his intervention in freeing them from slavery, the covenant with which he had always remained by their side. Now Jesus calls this wine the "blood of the covenant" or "of the new covenant."

Just imagine the astonishment of all present, who knew of only one untouchable covenant. It originated with the Exodus, at the dawning of the nation's history, and had been many times shattered by the people and many times renewed, but never taken away by God. Now that covenant is to be surpassed by a "new" one. Or rather, the old covenant reaches its fulfillment here, with this cup that is Christ's death and which now contains blood instead of wine.

God is not only faithful but takes us to new heights. Just as in the old covenant, God and Israel had committed themselves to one another through the blood of sacrifice, Ex 24, so in the new covenant God and humanity will be committed to one another through the sacrifice of love soon to be consummated on the cross.

Mt adds: "For the forgiveness of sins," 26:28. The meaning of Jesus' death is clear. It is the culminating act of redemption. It is God's definitive intervention on behalf of humanity. We can expect nothing greater as the events of the Calvary show us.

Biblical references permeate Jesus' language during the Supper. He is at the center of everything in every sense: cosmic, chronological, historical, meta-historical, salvific. In his human-divine love he accomplishes a round-trip departing from eternity, entering into history, and returning to eternity with the involvement of creation and especially of humanity. His words are very simple and human, taken from everyday life: bread, wine, eat, drink, body, blood, death, life; at the same time they are divine: bless, thank, covenant, forgiveness of sins, giving of one's life.

*O my Jesus, during the Supper you completely reveal God's plans for humanity. Now, the adventure you began with us is clear. If I look back, I can find meaning in all your deeds.*

The Eucharist, on its own account, is efficacious insofar as it is an act of Jesus himself. In practice, however, it can be rendered useless if the energy it contains is not harnessed and we lack the commitment to use it to spur us on to give our lives for others. I promise to examine how true this is of my life by comparing how often I receive the Eucharist with my commitment to acts of charity.

## SCENE 8: THE CENTRALITY OF THE EUCHARIST

At the Last Supper Jesus reveals the meaning of the death to which he is going to hand himself over. He gives his life, his body and blood, for the salvation of humanity. Salvation means covenant, friendship and solidarity with God and among one another.

This meaning is not only revealed, but it is also entrusted to a ritual such that it will remain alive and accessible in the community so that all can join in its celebration. It is the Eucharist.

The Eucharist goes beyond the ritual which perpetuates it in history. In fact, at the end of the Supper Jesus says: "I tell you, I shall not drink again of this fruit of the vine until the day when I drink it anew with you in my Father's kingdom," Mt 26:29. In Lk, this same comment falls between the two phases of the Supper, the Hebrew and the Christian.

Jesus' conclusion reveals two more facts.

First: he will die, but this does not mean that we will celebrate the Eucharist without him. After his resurrection he will once again preside at the meal with us from the kingdom of his Father. "With you," specifies Mt. The Eucharist will always remain his table, his gift of life. It will remain in history so that we may include in it the gift of our own lives. No longer will we say: "Let us eat this bread and drink this wine in remembrance of Egypt." Instead we will say: "Let us eat this bread and drink this wine in remembrance of Jesus," who remains with us, so that we also may be able to give our lives for others.

Second: the Eucharist, as ritual, will come to an end at the end of time and history, but it will continue as a sharing of life and love with God and among ourselves. The Eucharist on earth is a prelude to, or a rehearsal of paradise. Paradise is the Eucharist fulfilled.

In synthesis, the Eucharist we receive today is connected to the old covenant because it brings it to completion. It is projected towards the eternal covenant which in turn will be the Eucharist's fulfillment. It gives meaning and fullness to our present lives because it is communion with God and with our fellow human beings. It is an event which never ceases to exist because it must sustain the events which do pass away. Everything is born, grows, lives and dies, begins and ends. The Eucharist prolongs the Paschal Mystery on earth; it will find completion in eternity.

It is the event of all events. All others are linked to it and receive fullness of meaning from it. To the pagans who wanted to dissuade Christians from Sunday gatherings, since the beginning the Christians responded: *Sine Dominico esse non possumus*, i.e: We would not exist without the Sunday Eucharist.

It is impossible to be Christians without the Eucharist. Having received baptism, confirmation and matrimony is not enough. Sacraments must be lived out. This can happen only if they remain rooted in the Sunday Eucharist.

*O Jesus, you are one with God and one with us. You brought into our midst love which was only in God. Strengthen our faith, hope and charity, so that we may welcome God's love and feel it within us.*

I must examine how I live my life between Eucharists. If my life is consistent with the Eucharist, then it will be a preparation of gifts and a sacrifice of myself in gift for others. I must remember the Eucharistic sacrament by visiting Jesus, at least spiritually, in the tabernacle.

## SCENE 9: A STOP AND GO FELLOWSHIP

Predictions of failure in the following of Jesus frame the intimate atmosphere of the Supper. It begins with the denunciation of the betrayer. It ends with the prediction of abandonment and denial. How strange it is that when love reaches its highest point, so does the inability to understand love because it comes from the cross.

After the last canticle of the Supper, Jesus abruptly says: "This night you will all lose faith in me," Mt 26:31. His followers will all scatter. The Passion will shake the faith of the disciples and it will be, for the moment, a scandal, that is, an insurmountable obstacle. Jesus' adherence to his message and his faithfulness to the Father in sacrificing himself to save the world are now stumbling blocks, and grounds for separation and denial.

When Jesus does not conform to the preconceived image of what the Messiah would be like, everyone is scandalized. This was the case with his fellow Nazarenes and with the Pharisees who could not understand his teachings. Now, even his closest friends fall prey to this. The shepherd who sacrifices his life for his sheep finds that his disciples are so unprepared that, disillusioned, they disperse.

In the background we can almost see the Christian communities who were the recipients of the Gospel accounts, faced with difficulties in their following of Christ. We also find in it a warning for Christians: Following Jesus may be beautiful, but it is by no means easy. Fidelity presents many obstacles, of which the cross is always the greatest. In fact, according to Mt and Mk, the cross can destroy an unsteady faith.

"But after I am raised up, I will go before you to Galilee," Mt 26:32. Jesus' resurrection will restore faith. That fellowship which died with the scandal of the Passion will also be resurrected. It will happen in Galilee, a place of their most vivid experiences and heartfelt feelings. There the disciples were called and sent on a mission. There they became disciples. There they were taught and loved by the teacher. There they would receive their reward after the tumult of the Passion.

Lk does not insist on the wholesale defection of the disciples. While he does not hide their weaknesses, he maintains that they remain with Jesus, even if at a distance. During the Supper, Jesus says to them, "You are the ones who stayed with me in my trials; as my Father has granted me dominion, so I grant dominion to you," 22:28-29.

Their following of Jesus is safe, even though it had its ups and downs and periods of darkness.

Such is the mystery of the frailty of humankind and the turbulent nature of the cross. If despair does not engulf us, there is always the possibility of recovery.

*O Jesus, I must revisit my relationship with the cross. As I progress in my meditation on your Passion, help me to rediscover the love it contains so that I can better understand it.*

Becoming scandalized by the cross does not always mean apostasy from Christ or refusal to believe. The scandal of the cross can also infiltrate our lives on a daily level: by our non-acceptance of a place, of people, of an unexpected circumstance, of a word, of an illness. I must identify the cross, which I so often try to avoid, and resolve to carry it with love.

## SCENE 10: PETER'S RELUCTANCE TO ACCEPT THE CROSS

Mt is the evangelist who follows Peter in detail. Peter is always exalted but always inadequate. He wants to walk on the water but then begins to sink. He recognizes Jesus' divinity, but is then scolded and called Satan. He thinks he is being generous by saying he is ready to forgive seven times, but Jesus asks for seventy. He assures Jesus he will die with him, but then denies him on the first occasion. It is clear from his initial confession in Caesarea that his problem is the cross. When Jesus speaks of it for the first time, Peter calls him aside and rebukes him: "God forbid, Lord! This shall never happen to you," Mt 16:22.

Now that Jesus predicts that all of them will be scandalized, Peter jumps in with another bravado: "Even if all the others lose faith in you, I will never fall away," Mt 26:33. "I am ready to go with you to prison and to death," Lk 22:33. "I will lay down my life for you," Jn 13:37.

Jesus warns him of the emptiness of his words: "Truly, I say to you, this very night, before the cock crows, you will deny me three times," Mt 26:34. Impossible: "Even if I must die with you, I will not deny you," v. 35.

Peter refuses to accept Jesus' prophetic words. He has more faith in himself than he does in Jesus. He tried silencing Jesus when he spoke of the cross. Now it is Jesus who cautions him to be wary of stating that he will accept the cross. Jesus will carry his to the end. Peter will be incapable of following Jesus by accepting and carrying his own cross. Therefore, he will deny him.

According to Mt and Mk the other disciples echo Peter's bragging. All are deaf to Jesus' admonition that the cross is hard to bear. They do not ask for help or mercy.

Lk throws a gleam of light on our understanding of why Peter will eventually be saved. "Simon, Simon, behold, Satan demanded to have you, that he might sift you like wheat, but I have prayed for you that your faith may not fail; and when you have turned again, strengthen your brothers," 22:31-32. He will not be saved by his pretentiousness, but by the prayer of Jesus.

Satan, who already possesses Judas, will try to snatch them all; he will whirl them in the air as a farmer sifting wheat. Aggressive and rapacious, he will attempt to separate them all from Jesus.

Jesus reverts to calling Peter by his old name, Simon, perhaps to indicate that his identity is at risk, as are his faith and fellowship.

Jesus' prayer prevails over Satan's machinations. The many tempests he has let loose will come crashing down on this barrier, but will not shatter it. Peter's fall is frightful, but he will get back up, and he will once again be the rock, as Jesus announced.

We do not know the limits of our own weaknesses. We cannot tell to what point we are prepared to accept the cross in our lives. We must have faith in Jesus' prayers for us, and in the communion we share with him, especially through the sacrament of the Eucharist.

*O Jesus, thank you for praying for me. Your prayer is my anchor.*

Jesus' admonitions regarding the hardships of the cross oblige me to reexamine the virtue of humility. My strengths, convictions and abilities are important and are God's gift to me, but they are not enough. I need God by my side.

## SCENE 11: THE PASSION, A STRUGGLE

Lk inserts the narrative of the Last Supper within Jesus' farewell address. The Supper and the address end at the same time. As Jesus takes leave of his disciples, his last words echo those of when he had earlier sent them out on their mission. There is a mission involved here as well; in fact, it is an epilogue to the earlier one.

Preaching God's kingdom is always difficult because it comes into conflict with the opposition, which is Satan's reign.

In the past, the disciples were sent out without purse, bag, or sandals and still lacked for nothing, for the power of the word was sufficient and Jesus was always by their side. "But now," Jesus tells them, "let whoever has a purse take it; and likewise a bag. And let whoever has no sword sell his cloak and buy one," 22:36.

With this command Jesus warns of the final encounter with the forces of evil. He confirms that Satan is sifting through them as one sifts wheat. This epilogue will require special defensive equipment. Jesus will be taken from them. The word will be silenced. Darkness will envelop all.

The purse, the bag, the cloak and the sword are all symbols. Later on, in fact, Jesus, fully displeased because of their persistent lack of understanding, will halt the use of an actual sword with the sharp rebuke: "No more of this."

In his Gospel Lk uses the sword in a figurative sense in general to indicate sorrow and division. The prophet Simeon, in the temple, had predicted to Mary, the mother of Jesus, that a sword would pierce her own heart, 2:35. Jesus himself says that he did not come to bring peace, but rather the sword. Lk substitutes "sword" with the word "division," 12:51.

With the Supper coming to a close, Jesus once again tries to instill in his disciples an awareness of the frightful conflict which is about to take place. It will cause suffering, and attempt to divide and sever their unity. Therefore, they must be suitably armed.

Here again light is shed on the effect of the Passion on those involved and the danger they were in of being swept away.

*O my Jesus, I realize that I may never be thoroughly ready for the Passion and for the cross. I ask that by following you I may better prepare myself for it.*

By the Supper's end I have received sufficient light to understand Jesus' love for me. What about my love for him?

# Act II

# Gethsemane

    *For some exegetes, the Passion narrative begins in the garden of Gethsemane with the arrest. Thus, they exclude Jesus' prayer and struggle before he gives himself to the forces of darkness.*

    *Again, we will follow both liturgy and tradition. We deem Jesus' prayer in the garden of Gethsemane to be one of the most fruitful themes for meditation.*

    *The act is comprised of two parts: his prayer and his arrest.*

# I. JESUS' PRAYER

Mt 26:36-46     Mk 14:32-42     Lk 22:39-46     Jn 18:1

## SCENE 1: SOLITUDE DESPITE COMPANY

**Reflect.** The scene changes from the Upper Room to the garden of Gethsemane, or oil-mill, on the western slope of the Mount of Olives. When Jesus is in Jerusalem he often withdraws to this garden to pray. Lk notes that "the disciples followed him," 22:39, without further details. He sets up the scene as if it were a lesson on prayer; the teacher goes and his disciples follow to learn. The lesson during the Supper ends and the one in the garden begins. In Jn, also, the disciples follow Jesus to the garden, but the prayer scene is not described.

In Mt and Mk, Jesus enters the garden with the whole group, but he chooses three of them to remain closer to him. They are Peter, James and John, who have a special bond with the teacher. They were among the first to be chosen, they were present at the transfiguration, and at the resurrection of Jairus' daughter, they had difficulties with the discourse about the cross, together with Andrew they listened to Jesus' final discourse which warned: "Be on guard," Mk 13:37.

We do not know why these disciples are chosen. Perhaps because the experience of glory they had at Jesus' side would be incomplete without the experience of weakness and pain. Perhaps also for Jesus' human need to have someone close at hand at the hour of tragedy. Most certainly, because of his desire to prepare them for the approaching test.

Mt focuses on the need to have someone close by: "Stay here, and watch with me," 26:38. Later, Jesus' lament will be: "So, could you not watch with me one hour?" 26:40.

31

From the beginning of the Passion, Jesus expresses the need to be with his disciples. To celebrate the Passover "with my disciples," 26:18; to drink or eat again "with you in my Father's kingdom," v. 29. It is as though he cannot do without his disciples, as if he cannot pray without them.

While Jesus feels the need to be with them, they do not feel the need to be with him. The chosen three, along with the others, will not stay awake, but will fall asleep. Jesus will receive no comfort from his friends.

In certain cases, company can make us feel more alone than solitude itself. On the other hand, solitude can make us feel in companionship with the world we love. For Jesus this is certainly the case.

The disciples' sleep in the garden of Gethsemane does not really indicate their inability to keep Jesus company, but the lack of vigilance in the decisive moments of salvation. This is a very real risk for all humans. It is the dramatic temptation, as Jesus will soon call it.

**Pray.** *O Jesus, free me from the risk of falling asleep spiritually. If I don't feel the need for prayer, if I have lost the meaning of sin, if I do not commit myself to doing good whenever possible, then this has already happened.*

**Promise.** The garden of Gethsemane reminds me to be consistent in my choices. If I have chosen to be with Jesus, I cannot fall asleep, that is, live a life free of commitment, as if I belong to no one. To keep Jesus company means to build my life on his values.

## Scene 2: The prayer

According to Mt and Mk, Jesus begins his prayer in a state of extreme prostration, both physical and psychic. "He began to be upset and troubled. Then he said to them: 'My soul is greatly distressed, even to the point of death; remain here and watch with me.' And going a little farther he fell on his face and prayed," Mt 26:37-39.

"He began to be greatly distressed and troubled. And he said to them: 'My soul is very sorrowful, even to death; remain here and watch.' And going a little farther, he fell on the ground and prayed," Mk 14:33-35.

Lk expresses the state of Jesus' soul in gentler terms. He "knelt down" and prayed, 22:41. But his interior tension is indicated by the word "agony," that is the supreme struggle of the whole person. Fortunately the Revised Standard Version did not eliminate the word "agony," as other translations did, replacing it with "anguish," thus losing an important connotation in the text and in devotion.

The Synoptics note that the prayer is repeated and insisted upon. In Mt and Mk three times, a sign of perfection. Lk says: "He prayed more earnestly," 22:44. Only Mt has two different formulations: "My Father, if it be possible, let this cup pass from me; nevertheless, not as I will, but as you will," 26:39. "My Father, if this cannot pass unless I drink it, your will be done!" 26:42. The third time, the same words are repeated.

The difference between the first and the second formulation allows us to see the progression of the psychological adaptation of the human will to the unpleasant and repulsive event which is death.

Jn does not speak of the prayer in the garden of Gethsemane, but there are echoes of it in 12:27-29, at the moment of Jesus' glorification: "Now is my soul troubled. And what shall I say? 'Father, save me from this hour'? But it was for this that I have come to this hour. Father, glorify your name!"

This prayer scene is one of the most touching of the Passion. It is impossible to fathom the human-divine abyss of Jesus' prayer. It expresses his unique rapport with the Father as they deal with the unique mission of the incarnate Word, to save the world.

The supplication begins with a lament to the Father, a title which Jesus can use without equal. Mt prefers it; in fact, he uses it up to fifty-three times. In Mk, it becomes Abbà, like dad, a diminutive of Ab, which indicates the intimacy of family and a childlike abandonment, but also obedience and reverence.

The petition contains two objectives, one subordinate to the other: that the cup be taken away, and that the will of the Father be done. The cup signifies death.

What has happened? He who so loved the Father, he who has always looked to and exalted the will of the Father, to the point of making it his own nourishment, he who desired the cup as an opportunity to express to the fullest his love for the Father and for humanity, has now been plunged into fear and anguish, trembling, prostrate, his face to the ground.

The clash is not between Jesus' human and divine will, but between the human will and human sensitivity assumed by Jesus. The latter trembles and reacts because life is being taken away. According to the mystics the weakness of Jesus may be explained by the fact that he had a vision of the world's sin. This view was so oppressive that it was not humanly possible to endure. Perhaps. The experience of the saints can often be a source that helps us to understand the word of God.

The evangelists see in Jesus the Righteous One of Israel or the Servant of God who expresses his confidence in God also through prayers of lamentation, in the most dramatic of moments: betrayal by friends, prevailing of enemies, death's ambush without escape. God remains the sole refuge. Jesus is man. We do not know all of the consequences of his likeness to us. Some ancient writings considered this detail as unbecoming for the Son of God. But it is here, to remind us how terrible it is to die, and how prayer can make even death acceptable.

*O Jesus, thank you for having descended deep into the abyss of our frailty and for having taught us that prayer can help us rise up after every fall.*

In my prayer of petition I must ask God for two things: for the assistance I need, and that the Father's will be done. The first is subordinate to the second.

## SCENE 3: THE TEMPTATION

In contrast to Jesus' zeal for prayer is the estrangement of the sleeping disciples. It is impossible to awaken them.

In Mt and Mk, the three moments of Jesus' prayer alternate with three visits to his friends who are but a stone's throw away, not so much in search of solace, but to continue warning them of the test which will soon shake them violently. They do not wake up. Just as Jesus' prayer is perfect, so the disciples' failure is total. They no longer exist as disciples. Their bond with Jesus is broken. What follows in the Passion confirms this.

Lk tries to excuse them, saying that they were "sleeping out of grief," 22:45. Mk is pitiless: "Their eyes were very heavy; and they did not know what to answer him," 14:40.

The Synoptics agree on Jesus' intention to make sure the disciples would be prepared: "Watch and pray that you may not enter into temptation," Mk 14:38. Lk repeats the warning at the beginning and at the end of Jesus' prayer. Mt and Mk allege the reason for the urgency: "The spirit indeed is willing but the flesh is weak." Spirit and flesh do not indicate the components of the human being as body and soul, but the two opposite tendencies, wrestling within each person and subjected to the influence of temptation. Without prayer it is impossible to prevail in the struggle between the spirit and the flesh. Temptation is led by Satan. Alone, we are unfit for the struggle against him.

The disciples are not evil or unbelieving, but they are defenseless, at the mercy of the temptation which is on its way and which has already seized Jesus. Even in the garden of Gethsemane, the theme of the temptation is set against the Father's will. On the road to God's will there is always Satan, ready to provoke an incident. Also in the prayer of the Our Father Jesus warned us about this.

Satan tried to stop Jesus with the temptations in the desert. Lk had foretold that he would return to attack. He returns mainly in the Passion. He already has taken hold of Judas, but he is also after Jesus, fearful and in anguish in the face of death. Soon he will be after the disciples and will scatter them like chaff, because they are not praying.

Temptation against God's will signifies temptation to flee the cross. For Jesus, for the apostles, for all of us. In whatever form it presents itself, or whatever aspect of life it attacks, it always consists in dissuading us from carrying the cross with Jesus.

God's will is the cross; it is a plan of love which culminates in the gift of life. The temptation is to flee God's plan in order to put one of our own into play, one of egoism and idolatrous self-management. Prayer leads us straight in the direction of the Father's will, conquering all temptation. Without prayer we are like a ship without an anchor, or a tent without pegs.

O *Jesus, "the spirit is willing but the flesh is weak," has become a proverb we repeat to justify situations. Instead, you wanted to teach us to resolve them by fortifying nature with prayer.*

I must examine my appreciation and practice of prayer. Salvation follows that road. We cannot overlook it. Only those who pray will be saved. It is the electrical plug attached to the socket of divine energy.

## SCENE 4: THE AGONY

Jesus' prayer in the garden of Gethsemane has a culminating moment. Lk indicates it by signaling an angel's intervention to comfort Jesus. "Being in agony he prayed more earnestly," 22:44.

The arrival of the angel indicates that this is an exceptional moment. The angel is always a bearer of news: Jesus' conception, birth, resurrection. What is being announced at this particular moment?

The concepts of agony and earnestness in Jesus' prayer tell us that Jesus has reached a maximum mental tension and his limit to resist physically. Agony means struggle, the supreme phase of the battle which can end in death. But generally, it denotes an athlete's or warrior's victory.

With whom is Jesus fighting? With Satan, with death, with the Father's will, with the world's sin, with the needs of humanity which must be saved? What is he experiencing within himself at this moment?

Heb 5:7-8 informs us that Jesus "offered up prayers and supplications with loud cries and tears" and that "although he was a Son, he learned obedience through what he suffered."

Words of supplication, loud cries and tears were the forms of prayer of pious Israelites. Jesus must have used them frequently throughout his life. Perhaps even in the garden of Gethsemane. But how did Jesus learn obedience from what he suffered?

Perhaps the experience in the garden is the moment in which Jesus the man "learns," that is realizes, in the crudest and most complete manner, the disastrous situation produced by sin on human beings. At his own expense, "through what he suffered," when facing death alone, he "understands" how difficult it is for us to accept death, to do God's will, to resist Satan's attacks, to implore strength from above. He understands how arduous certain choices may be for us, how difficult it is to accept a cross. How difficult faith can be, sometimes almost impossible.

He learns obedience. He agrees with the Father, in the logic of love, that it is right for him to die for us. Thus, he remains close to humanity's countless Gethsemanes. And when each of us happens to be there, Jesus can say to us: I am with you. I have been there too.

Through this adherence Jesus exhausts all the energies of his human estate, of his soul and body. "His sweat became like great drops of blood falling down upon the ground," Lk 22:44.

The devout imagination has perhaps magnified the physical importance of this observation by the evangelist who was a physician. But the scientific hypothesis of today offers an even more dramatic perspective. Lk does not say that Jesus sweat drops of blood, but that the sweat was "like" drops of blood.

Some medical considerations today maintain that Jesus in the garden of Gethsemane suffered a heart attack. Lk, not having our scientific knowledge nor the corresponding terminology, probably described in the way he did the typical cold sweat and piercing pain of the heart attack victim. This might explain Jesus' successive weakness and his rapid death on Calvary.

*O Jesus, thank you for your solidarity with me, for being close to me in all my own Gethsemanes. You suffered alone, so that I may never be alone. You lie in wait in all human Gethsemanes to meet us when we also must pass by there.*

I must examine my reactions and behavior in difficult situations: relationships, services or choices to make, sickness. Often I toss every which way to resolve them. Through my head go many ideas. I turn to everyone, perhaps even to fortune tellers. I forget to turn to God in prayer.


Scene 5: The victory

Prayer has produced its results. Finished praying, Jesus is ready to face his Passion and death. "Behold, the hour has arrived, and the Son of man will be handed over into the hands of sinners. Get up! Let us be going! See, the one who is to hand me over has come," Mt 26:45-46.

His prayer has been answered. Not that the cup pass from him, but that he be given the strength to drink from it. The Father's will is to be done in full harmony between the Father and the Son. Prayer has made Jesus vigilant and strong in the face of any temptation.

What about the disciples? They will be at the mercy of Satan, but Jesus' prayer will once again snatch them away, as Lk guarantees.

For the last time Jesus announces his Passion as a handing himself over to sinners. It is about to engulf him. Already, through the olive trees, the torch lights glimmer and the clinking of swords can be heard. The men who will arrest Jesus, led by Judas, are arriving.

Mt and Mk again call attention to the centrality of the moment. "The hour has arrived," Mt 26:45, Mk 14:41. Jesus called the Supper his "hour" also because in it he anticipated his Passion. Now, he calls the moment of his arrest and capture his hour too, Lk 22:53. The hour—*kairos*—strikes in the garden of Gethsemane.

In the Synoptics Jesus' hour is that of his death, the culmination of his mission. In Jn, his hour refers to his glorification. But it always belongs to the Passion. For Jesus and for us, the hour is always when the Father's will is done. It has a final realization, but is also partially fulfilled throughout one's life. Thus we can talk about Jesus' hour as taking place at the Last Supper, in the garden of Gethsemane, at the trial, on Calvary, at the resurrection, and at his glorious manifestation at the end of time.

The garden of Gethsemane is always a determining hour of human existence. It indicates the extreme situations, the key moments, the crossroads of life. We can be blocked by the temptation or come out of the agony ready to give our life. It does not matter if human weakness manifests itself in all its forms, as happened to Jesus. It is important to pray to not succumb. Prayer does not need to be logical. It is enough that it be human, like the Hebrew prayers of lamentation, which consist at times of inarticulate cries and stammers. It is human to look for comfort and to fear death. We must be wary of sleep. He who sleeps in the garden of Gethsemane will never be ready to carry the cross on Calvary.

*O Jesus, as I manage my life, above all as I make choices, help me to always remain on the path toward the "hour," which leads me to fulfill my destiny according to the will of God.*

I must be aware that all the moments of life—things that happen, people I meet—may be the hour in which God calls and saves, when he wants to involve me in his plan of salvation.

# II. JESUS' ARREST

Mt 26:47-56      Mk 14:43-52      Lk 22:47-53      Jn 18:2-11

## SCENE 1: THE IMPOSTOR'S KISS

**Reflect.** Jesus' arrest is not secondary nor is it mentioned merely to link facts, but it is as important as all the other phases of the Passion. In all dramas of violence and death, including the stories of martyrs, the moment of the arrest is crucial, often more determining than the execution itself.

The prey is seized or the danger terminated, with the possible collaboration of spies or informers. Think of the kidnappings during ethnic wars or of the chronicles of terrorism in which doors are broken down in the middle of the night with cars screeching as they speed through the streets. These are always strong elements in police dramas and their presentations in film and TV. Jesus' arrest stirs up similar emotional feelings.

The Synoptics link together Jesus' prayer and his arrest. While Jesus is still speaking to alert the sleeping disciples, the one of the twelve who has hatched the conspiracy reappears. All of the Gospels speak of the signal of the kiss, but in Lk it appears as if Jesus does not permit it to be carried out. "He drew near to Jesus to kiss him," but the teacher reveals his plot as if to say that it is of no surprise: "Judas, would you betray the Son of Man with a kiss?" 22:47-48.

Instead, in Mt, Judas embraces Jesus and seals the kiss with a cold and detached greeting: "Hail, Rabbi!" "Peace, Rabbi," in the NRSV, 26:49. As during the Supper, he calls him neither Teacher nor Lord which would imply a bond of affection. Jesus

41

responds by recalling their past relationship: "Friend, why are you here?" 26:50. His question about betraying the Son of Man with a kiss is obscure. It can mean: You really *are* convinced about what you are doing, betraying me with a kiss!

The kiss could also have been a normal greeting between teacher and disciple. There are similar instances in the Bible. But how is it possible to use this sign of affection and life as a signal of death? There is no surprise on the part of Jesus, only hurt.

Jn never makes reference to the traitorous kiss, but paints the betrayal with powerful colors, starting with Jesus' discourse on the bread of life: "One of you is a devil," 6:70.

In the anointing at Bethany, Jn comments in much the same way regarding Judas' protest that the oil had been wasted: "This he said, not that he cared for the poor but because he was a thief, and as he had the money box he used to take what was put into it," 12:6. In the washing of the apostles' feet Jesus specifies that they are cleansed "but not all," 13:10.

During the Last Supper Jn denounces the presence of the betrayer as an unbearable affront: "The devil had already put it into the heart of Judas Iscariot, Simon's son, to betray him," 13:2. Quoting the Scriptures, Jesus affirms: "He who ate my bread has lifted his heel against me," 13:19. And further on he says: "One of you will betray me," 13:21. Upon the request to be more precise, Jesus indicates: "It is he to whom I shall give this morsel when I have dipped it," 13:26. From the terminology used some deduce that the morsel referred to was the Eucharist which, besides revealing love at its highest, can also manifest extreme alienation. In fact, the apostle Paul will say that whoever eats it without recognizing the Lord, "eats and drinks judgment upon himself," 1 Cor 11:29.

Except for Mt who will follow him to the end, the evangelists abandon Judas at this point. He has been identified with the darkness of the night and evil. He seems like a marionette in Satan's hands. But he is not.

**Pray.** *O Jesus, I worry too much about sinners' sins and I forget about the sins of friends, of believers, practicing Christians, and ministers who do not love enough and do not irradiate goodness.*

**Promise.** I must be vigilant not to pollute my relationship with others with hypocrisy. With God it is useless, but with others it can become a way of life. We can betray with a smile and a hug. We can hurt in an off-handed manner, unaffected, without feeling or pretending not to feel.

## SCENE 2: NOT AN AMBUSH BUT A HANDING OVER

Unexpectedly, the garden of Gethsemane fills with an unusual crowd. How many people? How much is reality and how much is symbolism in the narratives of the evangelists?

There is a mysterious destiny related to this geographical strip facing Jerusalem, from which, at sunset, one enjoys a breathtaking view of the temple and of the city. According to the Bible, David, disheartened by Absalom's revolt and Ahithophel's betrayal, finds refuge here. From here Jesus will ascend into heaven and here he will return in glory. Here, God will gather humanity for the universal judgment. The "hour" of prayer and of Jesus' arrest only add to the place's significance.

This night, possibly lit by the moon, the men who will arrest Jesus pour in, "a large crowd with swords and clubs," Mt and Mk. "A crowd" among which were "the chief priests and captains of the temple and elders," Lk 22:47, 52. "So Judas, procuring a band of soldiers and some officers from the chief priests and the Pharisees, went there with lanterns and torches and weapons," Jn 18:3.

Each narrator arranges the adversaries according to the degree of aggressiveness and rejection of Jesus that he wants to express—an anonymous and unspecified crowd for Mt and Mk; including the supreme heads of the Jewish nation according to Lk; even the Jewish and Roman militia according to Jn who also mentions the torches, whose light contrasts with the night.

The Roman cohort was one tenth of the six thousand soldiers of the legion, thus 600 men. Even if only a maniple, 60 or 120 soldiers, was called into service it remains an exaggeration. Perhaps Pilate had consented to Jesus' arrest and sent reinforcements. If you add to these the guards of the Jewish militia who were at service at the temple, the whole affair would appear more like the conquest of a city.

Even if this marshaling of troops is improbable from an historical point of view, it expresses in an eloquent manner the blinding effect of rejecting Jesus. Opposition to love is always tragic and at the same time ridiculous. Irony dominates the situation, as Jesus highlights: "Have you come out as against a robber, with swords and clubs to capture me?" Mt 26:55.

The animosity was brewing, but it did not dare express itself openly for fear of the people who were following Jesus. Now, however, it is possible to do something, thanks to Judas, his betrayer, and to the protection offered by the cover of darkness.

As an ambush, this is certainly no masterpiece. The soldiers go to abduct him and he is there, waiting for them, already aware of everything that was about to transpire. They go out with an army and they do not even find any bodyguards. Readers of the Gospels expect an explanation of Jesus' passivity. Here it is: fulfillment of the Scriptures; the hour of darkness; Jesus' free will of abandonment of himself to death out of love.

*O Jesus, the forces of evil always need exaggeration, choreography, to make an impression and gain power. Instead, good often appears as if it were nonexistent. And yet good is the strength that counts. It is like you in the hour of darkness.*

It is of no use to try to combat evil with evil. Evil is defeated by the love of Jesus. It dies when, venting itself, it finds resistance in love. This is the essence of Jesus' Passion. I must understand it.

## SCENE 3: AN ENDLESS CONFLICT

Jn's Gospel reads like the narration of an uninterrupted trial against Jesus. On several occasions his adversaries even pronounce the death sentence against him and gather stones to throw at him, but they do not dare to do more for fear of the people who support him. In addition, he always confutes their incriminating arguments.

The moment of the arrest is the opportunity for another

episode of the polemic. Jn prepares the confrontation with care, always adhering to his preference for contrasts.

On one side is Jesus with his small group. On the other are his opponents: Judas, Jewish power with its leaders and Roman power with its army. Unarmed and sure of himself, Jesus causes a shiver of anxious stupor to run through the crowd at his mere presentation of himself. "Then Jesus, knowing all that was to befall him, came forward and said to them: 'Whom do you seek?' They answered him: 'Jesus of Nazareth.' Jesus said to them: 'I am he.' Judas who betrayed him was standing with them. When he said to them: 'I am he,' they drew back and fell to the ground," 18:4-6. Judas is also on the ground with the others.

No show of strength, imposing as it may be, can oppose itself to the power of Jesus' love. The power of darkness shrinks in the presence of God's love, even when it may appear to be winning.

Jesus' self-revelation is beautiful to those who accept his love, but dreadful to those who refuse it. It is not enough to repudiate it in order to shield oneself from its existence and its call.

Jesus repeats the question to settle another issue before handing himself over. His opponents must not do any more damage than consented to: "If you seek me, let these men go," 18:8. He is ready for the test because he has prayed. In Jn 17, this prayer took place at the Supper, during Jesus' marvelous invocation to the Father. "These men," the disciples, instead have slept. Put to the test, they may apostatize and betray him. They are not yet ready to become martyrs.

Jesus had asked and promised the Father that none of his would be lost. His prayer now becomes a strategic intervention, a negotiation with power to make sure that it does not surpass its limits.

Love for others must not be limited to prayer, even though prayer is essential.

*O Jesus, thank you for having revealed to me that love always wins, even when it is rejected, not because it makes us collapse to the ground, but because it is the power of God.*

When I am rejected or unrecognized I must not worry about claiming respect by defending myself from accusations. I must only be concerned with continuing to love.

## SCENE 4: STOP THE VIOLENCE

Someone tries to defend Jesus with the use of arms. An ear of the chief priest's servant is severed. For Mk, the blow comes from "one of those who stood by," 14:47, insinuating that it might be one of the aggressors in the scuffles provoked by the counter-offensive. Mt however clarifies that the assault comes from "one of those who were with Jesus," 26:51. Jn gives him a name: it is "Simon Peter, having a sword," uses it with his usual impetuosity, 18:10.

Jn also names the unfortunate victim, Malchus. Lk and Jn say that the right ear has been severed. This detail leads us to suspect that this may be a legally serious mutilation, which could have resulted in an inability to serve in the temple. The healing worked by Jesus may be a gesture of social reintegration.

Jesus disapproves of the use of arms. He cites a current proverb: "Put your sword back into its place; for all who take up the sword will perish by the sword," Mt 26:52. This is more than simple passivity; it is being consistent with Jesus' teachings on non-violence and forgiveness.

Violence starts chain reactions which do not cease. Jesus has already denounced the useless violence of aggressors; how could he defend the violence of the victims? He is against all violence of both the offending and the defending party. He repudiates the methods and the values of the world dominated by sin.

It is Jesus' final teaching as a free man. In fact, according to the Synoptics, he may have been hunted down by his enemies, but he has not yet been taken away. Handcuffed and chained, it is as if he were still on the pulpit "seated in the temple," confirming his theme on non-violence, in accord with his discourse on the mountain. This teaching is not a social tactic, but an essential element of the new commandment of love. His adversaries deceive themselves into believing that they have him in their hands and that they have rendered him harmless, but he is still a "revolutionary."

The gesture of reattaching the ear confirms the words: violence must not only be avoided, it must be repaired. If it cannot be stopped quickly, even before it starts, it becomes almost impossible to avoid it or to make reparation.

In Jn, Jesus shows that he can defend himself on his own. In Mt, he brings forth the hypothesis of his Father's assistance, who could send him "more than twelve legions of angels," 26:53. The Father can provide for his own Son better than anyone. But the Father's desire, already made clear in the Scriptures, calls for another way. "Shall I not drink the cup which the Father has given me?" Jn 18:11.

Salvation cannot proceed through human means. It can use them, but only if adapted to express God's love. Violence can never do this. Humanity must understand this if it is to realize any level of growth.

*O Jesus, your love is an energy more powerful that any violence.*

Violence can destroy one's spiritual life just as surely as impurity and pride. It nestles even in the hearts of so-called "good" men and women and is powerful as that which provokes massacres and wars. Wounds that do not heal, forgiveness that is not willingly given or asked for, result in violence. It is necessary to uproot on time all signs of violence.

## SCENE 5: THE ICON OF THE PASSION

At the end of the Gethsemane scenario Jesus is alone in the hands of the enemy. Lk does not mention this because it would lessen his emphasis on the failure of the followers of Jesus, and Jn omits it because it does not suit the majesty of the Jesus of his report, but darkness now dominates the events, as does the night which closes in.

Mk adds another case of a disappearing follower. An aspiring disciple had slipped into the garden. Perhaps he was a curious young man or a candidate of the Lord. He is arrested along with Jesus. Since he had wrapped himself in a linen cloth for sleeping purposes, he sheds it, and leaving it in the hands of the soldiers, escapes naked into the night.

Some scholars have suggested that it might have been Mk himself or the young man of the resurrection. Thus the Passion, from its beginning, already foreshadows its conclusion. Perhaps the linen cloth is a symbolic allusion to the white baptismal gown.

Knowing Mk and his straightforward style, it may well be another symbol of the disciples' radical abandonment and of Jesus' solitude. At the beginning the disciples had left everything behind to follow Jesus: relatives, homes, work tools and material goods. Now they abandon everything, even their clothes, so as *not* to be involved with Jesus.

According to some scholars, for Jn the Passion begins here. Whatever the case, the arrest is one of the pivotal points of the Passion. It is the essential point of arrival and departure. Jesus is alone before the turning point of events, which are already prepared and anticipated.

The arrest is the Supper unfolding: Jesus' body is broken and handed over, it is given as a meal. The prayer in the garden of Gethsemane brings life and strength as the Father's will is done. Freedom is handed over, that is, used to the fullest, invested, not hoarded to do with as one wants.

In fact, Jesus is perfectly free: to speak, to keep silent, to allow himself to be taken away, condemned and killed. He is free to love to the very end. The person who is really under arrest is not Jesus, but those who drag him before the tribunal. They are prisoners of hatred.

The stage is set for that phase in which Jesus will accomplish all that he came to do. Under arrest, it appears that he cannot do much. Instead, the conclusion of his work is in process: he acts by not being able to act, by letting others act, by accepting what others do. He acts, not by doing but solely by being. His is the humble, simple being of every humiliated, rejected, sick and dying man or woman—the being of the cross.

*O Jesus, you show us that no abandonment by friends or any enemy's violence can destroy the dignity of a human being. Above all, nothing can take away from us the Father's company and protection.*

Do not be excessively afraid of solitude or abandonment. Instead, take care never to leave anyone feeling lonely. Never rob others of their dignity through rash judgment, prejudice or gossip.

# Act III

# The Trial

Given the goal of this work, we will skirt the complex historical and exegetical problems relative to Jesus' trial, and will mention them only when necessary to the setting of the scenes for our meditation.

Following his arrest, Jesus is subjected to the judgment of two different authorities: the religious-political one of the Jewish nation and the political one of the Romans, which, from a half a century before Christ, governed Palestine with diverse forms of dominion.

Before the Roman authority, a real trial takes place. Before the Jewish authority an interrogation was held, whose legal nature is not clear. According to the Synoptics it could have been a real juridical trial. According to Jn it certainly was not.

It is impossible to reconstruct with historical precision the character of this confrontation.

If it was a trial, what was its value? If it was not a trial, what on earth was it?

If it were a real trial, could it end with a sentence?

If yes, could the sentence have been executed?

The Jewish authorities tell Pilate that they cannot put anyone to death, but earlier on they had attempted on several occasions to stone Jesus, and later on they will stone Stephen to death. Perhaps at Jesus' time the rules fluctuated.

*If not a real trial, it was probably just a private interrogation, or a preliminary hearing to gather and formalize the accusations to be presented to the Roman authority in order to obtain the death sentence against Jesus.*

*We will continue our meditations by focusing on the message conveyed by the Gospels, rather than on these issues.*

*We will divide this act in two parts: the religious trial and the civil trial.*

# I. THE RELIGIOUS TRIAL

Mt 26:57-75    Mk 14:53-72    Lk 22:54-71    Jn 8:12-27

SCENE 1: IN SEARCH OF AN ACCUSATION

**Reflect.** Jesus' appearance before the Jewish authorities is the most complicated part of the Passion accounts. According to Mt and Mk, Jesus is quickly interrogated during the night at the high priest's residence. The hearing is then repeated the next morning before the Sanhedrin because the night meeting does not have legal value.

For Lk, only the morning gathering takes place. Mk and Lk do not mention the name of the high priest who is interrogating Jesus. Mt says that it is Caiaphas, who in fact, ruled from 18 to 37 A.D.

Jn reports that Jesus appears before Caiaphas, but he does not recount the interrogation. He does, however, say that Jesus is questioned during the night by Annas, the father-in-law of Caiaphas. We know that Annas had been high priest from 6 to 15 A.D. Deposed by the Romans, he retained great prestige and perhaps the Jews still considered his high priesthood to be valid. It is probable that Lk also implies that he is present, since he speaks of the interrogation of the high priests, plural.

The Synoptics end with a death sentence pronounced by the Sanhedrin against Jesus because of blasphemy. Jesus' attitude before this pronunciation is one of consistency and strength in Mt and Mk, of faith and abandonment to the will of the Father in Lk, and of supreme majesty in Jn.

The same message comes through clearly in all of the accounts: Jesus is innocent, so much so that no one is capable of proving him guilty. Jesus steadfastly proclaims his own identity, remaining faithful to himself and to the Father. The Jewish authorities reject Jesus.

The Sanhedrin is an assembly of seventy individuals plus a president. It includes high priests, elders and scribes, and is the highest religious and civil authority in the nation.

For Mt and Mk, the trial begins with an interrogation of the witnesses. The sole accusation is that Jesus had said: "I am able to destroy the temple of God and rebuild it in three days," Mt 26:61. Or: "I will destroy this temple that is made with hands, and in three days I will build another not made with hands," Mk 14:58. The evangelists note that both the witnesses and the charge are false. In fact, they are merely confused. Actually Jesus said: "'Destroy this temple, and in three days I will raise it up....' But he was speaking of the temple of his body," Jn 2:19, 21.

Jesus had used the terms "destroy" and "raise," but with reference to his own body as a temple and attributing to himself its reconstruction. He had always spoken of the stone temple with respect, but he also demonstrated that he was superior to it. He purified it by driving out those who were desecrating it and he predicted its end. Thus, the accusation may have had a pretext, but the witnesses manipulate what Jesus had truly said.

The confusion of the witnesses and the indifference demonstrated by Jesus, who speaks not a word to clarify or to defend himself, irritate the high priest. But the accusation regarding the temple has this effect—the high priest becomes suspicious. If Jesus claims power over the temple, then he must consider himself the Messiah, because only God and his messenger have this power.

Thus the crucial question revolves around Jesus' identity. Objectively there are no accusations which stand up. It is necessary to find something by provoking him into speaking. Their malicious intent sharpens the drama: Jesus will now be judged by his words, which can be nothing but truth, that truth which always frees, even from the attachment to life.

**Pray.** O *Jesus, they arrested you with the assurance of incriminating you without difficulty, but already they are confused as to how to make the accusations against you stick. Innocence may be forced to remain silent, but it cannot be destroyed.*

**Promise.** Sometimes to appear important or innocent I invent or exaggerate the faults of others. I must pay attention to this perverse mechanism of human relationships, which destroys friendships and family ties.


SCENE 2: IDENTITY ASSERTED

In Mt with a single phrase, in Mk with two questions, in Lk with two interrogations formulated by the entire Sanhedrin, in Jn with a fine disquisition on his disciples and on his doctrine, the attack to discover the identity of the accused is under way. "I adjure you by the living God, tell us if you are the Christ, the Son of God," Mt 26:63.

In the Synoptics the question has two connotations. First: Are you the Christ, that is, the awaited Messiah, the definitive liberator of the nation? Second: Are you the Son of God? Regarding the interpretation of the relationship between the Messiah and God there was no unanimity. It was important to the interrogators that they hear an answer to these two questions from the lips of Jesus himself.

For the readers of Mt and Lk, the answer was already clear, since the question contains the title with which Jesus and other figures in the Gospels—the Father, the disciples, the demons— had already expressed his identity. To repeat it meant to confirm it. But for Mk's audience, the answer would be a moment of maximum revelation, equal only to the one which will occur on Calvary with the proclamation uttered by the centurion after Jesus' death. Thus, Mk's scenario is more suggestive and touching. The question drops a bomb shell. The answer is the explosion.

The brief interval between the two brings to a climax the spiteful anticipation of the opponents. They have been waiting for some justification to unchain the hatred which weighs upon them. This time Jesus cannot keep silent because the question is formulated by legitimate authority with a lawful appeal to God.

The answer resonates in the palpable silence: "I am; and you will see the Son of Man sitting at the right hand of Power, and coming with the clouds of heaven," Mk 14:62.

The impression is enormous. For a moment everyone freezes. Even the most aggressive assuredness can vacillate. Never had Jesus been so clear. In Mk's Gospel, to avoid temporal interpretations, he had never willingly accepted these titles. But now that he is a prisoner and no longer can anyone equivocate, he welcomes them and confirms that they belong to him.

Moreover, he adds his favorite title: Son of Man. It is a mysterious term taken from the prophet Daniel. On the one hand it expresses his divine identity and activity, on the other it veils it by placing emphasis on his human nature. He comes on the clouds of heaven and judges the world, which is specific to God, but his title is "Son of Man," and thus it is possible to include the perspective of the cross.

The answer sends us back to the cross and explains Jesus' prudence in keeping veiled his own identity to this point. He cannot be understood until the purpose of his being on earth is understood, that is, to give his life for the salvation of humanity. The moment that will reveal fully who he is will, therefore, be that of the cross. Since he is now on the way to the cross, he can use the formula of God's self-revelations: I Am.

The cross, in turn, expresses God's judgment on history. It is pronounced on the cross as the supreme manifestation of love, and it will be completed at the end of time. At that time the victory of the Crucified One and the human response will be manifest to all.

*O Jesus, give all Christians the courage to profess their true identity.*

There is a popular atheism abroad that is more powerful than popular religiosity: it can be seen in sports, theatrical performances, rock concerts, the world of business and fashion, discos, universities and many cultural environments. Its celebrations are more attended than those of patron saints. God seems to be absent from them. How can I become involved to render him present? First of all, I can do this by not hiding my Christian identity.

## Scene 3: Identity refused

They asked their questions; they received their answer; now they reject it. They look for the truth, but they are not willing to accept it. Their refusal is expressed in various forms through words and gestures.

The death sentence is for reason of blasphemy: "'You have heard his blasphemy. What is your decision?' And they all condemned him as deserving death," Mk 14:64.

Mt and Mk both record the accusation of the crime of blasphemy and the resulting sentence. Lk takes into account only Jesus' testimony. According to Jewish law, blasphemy is a crime punishable by death; it refers to the sacrilegious use of God's name, cf. Lv 24:10-16. We cannot understand how the Sanhedrin so surely recognized this crime in Jesus' words.

The tearing of one's garments was a violent way of manifesting utter disapproval and rejection.

In Mt and Mk this death sentence is followed by the first series of insults against Jesus. "They spat in his face, and struck him; and some slapped him saying: 'Prophesy to us, you Christ! Who is it that struck you?'", Mt 26:67-68.

It is the members of the solemn Sanhedrin who have stooped to this level. Their insults are refined in their brutality. They laugh scornfully at Christ's messianic title and at his qualification as prophet. It is as if they were already executing the death sentence, destroying his dignity by contempt.

But Jesus is already realizing his mission of redemption through the love with which he accepts and gives of himself. He is insulted with his title of "Christ" and because of it. With this same title he will be invoked and loved for centuries.

In Lk the jibes are not related to the rejection of Jesus' identity; instead they precede the interrogation by the high priest. Perhaps they lasted all night long, from the arrest to the morning sitting of the Sanhedrin. The objective is to show the disciples that during his Passion Jesus is ready and at peace, because he has prayed in Gethsemane. Meanwhile Peter, close by, is denying the teacher. The rejection of the prophet contrasts with what is happening. The facts confirm that Jesus is truly a prophet, because he had predicted all this.

In Jn the rejection of Jesus' identity is expressed with a slap. When questioned regarding matters of doctrine and about his disciples, Jesus does not give a direct answer, but refers to public opinion. "I have spoken openly to the world; I have always taught in synagogues and in the temple. Why do you ask me? Ask those who have heard me, what I said to them; they know what I said," Jn 18:20-21.

Those present realize that Jesus does not answer because he considers the interrogator Annas, the high priest, incapable of accepting the truth. Perhaps the taunt is still ringing in their ears: "You are from your father the devil, and you long to do your father's desires. But because I speak the truth, you do not believe me," cf. Jn 8:44-47. Jesus is imperturbable, while all the rest feel awkward and ill at ease.

Since there is insufficient substance for scenes of execration, the response is expressed with a slap and a reproach by a soldier: "'Is that how you answer the high priest?' Jesus answered him: 'If I have spoken wrongly, bear witness to the wrong; but if I have spoken rightly, why do you strike me?'" Jn 18:22-23.

Thus the answer to the high priest is also clear. Jesus is the word which speaks the truth, reveals the Father and expresses love. But the reaction is rejection, much more dramatic than the shock of a slap. In Jn the slap expresses the same power of rejection as the scorns, the insults and the slaps in Mt and Mk.

*O Jesus, the more they try to reject you, the more it becomes evident that it is impossible to do so. If you are condemned for what you say, it means that you speak the truth.*

I must look out for the subtle forms of rejection of Jesus which infiltrate my life. They may take the form of egoism, falsehoods, the keeping up of appearances, attachment to projects or personal pleasures and may block my spiritual growth for life.

## SCENE 4: THE POWER OF WORDS AND THE POWER OF SILENCE

"'Have you no answer to make? What are these men testifying against you?' But Jesus was silent," Mt 26:62-63. "He was silent and made no answer," Mk 14: 61.

From time to time the evangelists call attention to Jesus' silence during the trials. This behavior has always touched the emotions of those who meditate on the Passion. From the beginning Christians have recognized in this silence two models of perfection present in the Bible: the Servant of God and the Righteous One of Israel.

The prophet Isaiah, in particular, speaks of the first: "He was oppressed, and he was afflicted, yet he opened not his mouth; like a lamb that is led to the shearers is dumb, so he opened not his mouth," Is 53:7. Other prophets, the psalms and the books of Wisdom speak of the second. His characteristic is that he always trusts in the Lord, silently putting up with even the most painful of trials.

Jesus' silence is striking not only because he does not take the provocations to himself, but mostly because he does not react to the arbitrary unfolding of the showdown. Trials, especially religious ones, are anomalies for many reasons. And Jesus keeps silent.

The botched hearing during the night, on the threshold of the paschal feast, was formalized at dawn without debate. The witnesses were encouraged to bear false witness, no matter how invalid their testimony was because they could not agree among themselves. The death sentence pronounced for a crime which is not legally clear precedes the handing over to the Roman authorities on grounds which remain equally obscure. All this is against international law, including rabbinical law. And Jesus keeps silent.

Worst of all are the ignoble volleys of the most distinguished leaders of the nation who allow themselves to destroy the most elementary dignity of an accused: by spitting in his face, blindfolding and beating him, and offending the values in which he most believes. And Jesus remains silent.

His silence is more powerful than any word, because it expresses love when speaking is no longer communication. The trial demonstrates this in various instances. Sometimes Jesus remains silent not because he has nothing to say or because he wants to give an example of mortification, but because the interlocutor does not want to communicate but merely wants to trap him or deny the truth.

For this reason he responds only when commanded to do so in the name of God. He explains to Annas that a direct answer is pointless and he defends himself when slapped by revealing the cowardice behind the violence. In Lk Jesus explicitly states: "If I tell you, you will not believe; and if I ask you, you will not answer," 22:67-68, thus providing an answer, which is readily rejected.

Words and silence are two means of communication to be used with prudence. To overuse words can inflate them, wear them out and make them meaningless.

*O Jesus, teach me to use silence more and words less as a means of communication and of closeness and understanding towards others.*

Today to communicate often does not mean to transmit values but rather to evade the truth and speak of that which is ephemeral. For a Christian, the Gospel, Jesus and his love must always be part of what is communicated. If my life does not do so, then I resolve to change.

## Scene 5: Peter, kamikaze of obstinacy

It seems like a piece of fiction penned by an experienced novelist. Is it possible that Peter actually behaved in such a manner? The evangelists elaborate on his behavior in scenes that can hardly be surpassed. They contain precious teachings. His story cannot be the fruit of anti-Peter sentiments in some early Church community.

The narration of the Gospels on this point proceed along the same lines: Jesus' questioning and that of Peter crisscross. Both are interrogated regarding their identity. The questions and answers are intertwined as is the clash of contrasts.

In Mt Peter follows Jesus from afar. He enters into the high priest's palace and sits in the courtyard.

According to the other evangelists he warms himself by a fire, whose flames facilitate recognizing him.

In Jn, he is able to enter thanks to the intervention of another disciple, perhaps the evangelist himself, who knows the high priest.

Among the questioners all include a serving-girl. Mt and Mk mention two of them. Peter is even afraid of them, whose testimony would not be relevant in a formal trial. For Mt, Mk and Jn, one of the questions comes from all those present. Lk, instead, has two men intervene, perhaps insinuating that their testimony has legal validity.

In the Synoptics, Peter is recognized by his Galilean accent. In Jn he is pointed out by a relative of Malchus who was present when Peter's sword slashed and cut off Malchus' ear.

He was trapped. Peter loses all control and his negations

explode like a grenade. Here is the sequence, according to each evangelist.

"He denied it in front of everyone and said, 'I don't know what you're talking about!'"—"And he denied it again with an oath: 'I do not know the man!'"—"Then he put himself under a curse and swore, 'I do not know the man!'" Mt 26:70-74.

"He denied it, saying: 'I neither know nor understand what you are saying.'"—"Again he denied it.—He put himself under a curse and swore an oath, 'I don't know the man you're talking about!'" Mk 14:68-71.

"He denied it, saying: 'Woman, I do not know him.'"—"Man, I am not."—"Man, I do not know what you are saying," Lk 22:57-60.

"He said: 'I am not.'"—"He denied it and said: 'I am not.'"—"Peter again denied it," Jn 18:17, 25-26.

Mt highlights the fact that the negation happens "in front of everyone." This is exactly the opposite of what Jesus had asked of his disciple: that they would recognize him in front of everyone.

The escalation of the denial is a tragic paradox: feigning, he denies Jesus; swearing, he denies him; swearing and cursing, he denies him. In Mk his apostasy is like a brush fire, accelerating so fast that he has no time to think and to protect himself. It begins with a face to face encounter with a serving-girl; it grows as she brings the fact to the attention of all those present and it explodes with their agreement. The accusations, as well as the denials, are built upon terminology related to belonging and fellowship. He denies everything.

Jn also reveals that denial destroys any bond of belonging to the community of the disciples and to Jesus. Both are essential and constitutive of his identity; yet Peter tears himself away from them as if they were obstructing encumbrances.

The message could not be any clearer. While the teacher, during the trial, is affirming his own identity and for this is rejected, the disciple, in the simplest exchange during the trial of his existence, denies his own identity as a follower of Jesus.

"I am," affirms Jesus. "I am not," echoes Peter.

O *Jesus, if Peter acts this way, what of me in my relationship of belonging and fellowship?*

Each day I must pray to remain faithful to Jesus. I must be watchful that I am such in all my actions, thoughts, choices and words. If the first pope can fall so disastrously, what will be of me, the last of Jesus' followers?

## SCENE 6: JESUS' LOOK AT PETER

According to Lk Peter's fall transmits other lessons as well. The disciple's failure is a counterpoint to the teacher's success, but the scene is connected to the Last Supper and to the garden of Gethsemane. Jesus' prediction, his promise of support, his warning to pray, and the imminent intervention of his reconciling glance resonate harmoniously. Coherence and incoherence, fidelity and infidelity are linked by prayer. He who prays succeeds; he who does not pray falters.

In Lk, the denial is attenuated. Peter does not disqualify himself to the point of cursing and swearing. In addition, all the interrogators say that he "too" is one of the disciples, insinuating that even the others of the group are around, watching over Jesus.

The denials are followed by the cock's crow. Indicated by Jesus' prophecy, it was the signal with which those who had night shifts, like soldiers, counted time. Mk is more precise than the others because he speaks of the second time the cock crows. We know that cocks crow at various times during the night. The first crow may have corresponded to three o'clock in the morning, and the second to four o'clock.

The shrill signal which pierces the night reminds Peter of Jesus' prediction. In Lk the return of awareness is caused not by the sound of the crow, but by Jesus' glance. "And the Lord turned and looked at Peter. And Peter remembered the word of the Lord," 22:61.

Let us not forget Lk's approach. It is Thursday night. Jesus has gone from the garden of Gethsemane to the palace of the high priest. He will be interrogated the next morning. Meanwhile he becomes a source of amusement for the soldiers who abuse him in the area of the courtyard where Peter is warming himself. Perhaps Jesus and Peter are within sight of one another. Jesus may have heard with his own ears the atrocity of his disciple. At a certain point, as he was being moved from one place to another, he exchanges glances with him.

In the Synoptics the scene concludes with Peter's tears. "And he went out and wept bitterly," Mt 26:75 and Lk 22:62. "And he broke down and wept," Mk 14:72.

Without a formal disquisition, but with a handful of narrative features, the evangelists present a treatise on Christology and on the spiritual life. We catch a glimpse of the first Christian communities beaten down by trials and persecutions. There are martyrs, it is true, but there are also apostates who fall out of fear. The authors tell not only of the sufferings and example of Jesus, but also of the crises of all those involved in the Passion. Everyone runs the risk of fleeing before the test. Any compromise is possible, including betrayal.

Peter's tears are tears of repentance, thus they allow him to be reconstituted in the integrity of his identity and mission. Jesus does not demean him but holds him to the task with which he had earlier entrusted him. Jesus is not embarrassed that the future support of other witnesses began with a failure in his own witness. Peter's fall and his repentance will be recounted throughout the world to say that this also is Gospel or good news: to always be rescued by love.

*O Jesus, weakness and sin must not make me lose faith in your love. Allow me to get used to your look which watches over me because, while confidence in my own strength is important, it is not enough without faith in the power of your love.*

In our society many people are like inflated balloons. Am I one of them? We may have obtained degrees or made some money and we no longer feel the need of anyone, not even God. Then, when faced with problems, we lose our sense of equilibrium and dignity. May Peter's fall and Jesus' understanding teach me humility and a sense of my limits.

## SCENE 7: JUDAS IN THE ABYSS

Judas does not open himself to the mercy of God but sinks into despair. Only Mt narrates the event, 27:3-10, using it to separate the religious trial from the civil one and to present a complete list of the actors in the drama. Lk recounts it in Acts 1:15-20, which we will take into consideration.

In the early morning, while Jesus is taken to the governor, Pontius Pilate, Judas lives out the final episode of his destiny. He, too, may have met the glance of the teacher during his transfer from one place to another. What is certain though is that he does not let himself be moved by it. Here again we witness profound theology narrated in a fast-paced scene.

Perhaps Judas expected that Jesus would escape captivity, but seeing that he was condemned by the Sanhedrin, the betrayer is taken by remorse and gives back the money, saying, "I have sinned in betraying innocent blood," Mt 27:4.

Then, seeing that his accomplices are not interested in such spiritual problems, he flings the money into the sanctuary and runs off to hang himself. The high priests do not use the money for sacred expenses since it was used to buy an innocent person. Instead, they use it to purchase a field in which to bury foreigners. For this reason the plot of land is called "Field of Blood."

Lk's version in the book of the Acts contains different elements. The field is purchased by Judas himself. His death appears to be more accidental than suicidal, but in a macabre and horrifying manner. The name of the field does not derive from Jesus' blood, bought with the same money, but from Judas' blood. Perhaps circulation of the episode by word of mouth has served to modify its contents, the two narrators having drawn from different sources.

The irony in Mt points to the high priests' insincerity. They pretend to be innocent. At the same time they recognize that an innocent person was bought with their money and put to death. They are paired with the betrayer. Later on, Pilate will also try to wash his hands of any complicity.

Down through the centuries many people will repeat this act, not wanting to appear responsible for Christ's betrayal when they betray one another or when they are not faithful to each other. It is useless to wash one's hands or to confiscate the substance of the offence. The imprint remains on our consciences and in our souls.

To blot it out, only Peter's way works, not Judas'. Mt elaborates a message with many lessons. He notes the contrast between Jesus' fidelity and Peter's infidelity, and the contrast between the pain which leads to repentance, and the remorse which leads to despair. There is a grief that is resolved, because it is open to repentance and to the acceptance of forgiveness. And there is a grief that is unresolved, that is closed, that kills oneself and others.

Repentance rebuilds all; despair destroys all. Peter "went out and wept bitterly," Mt 26:75. Judas "went out and hanged himself," Mt 27:5.

Judas disappears from the Passion after having greatly influenced it. Why did the evangelists leave us so many details of him? Did similar cases continue to occur within the community? It is not to be excluded. But the emphasis is on the seriousness of being a follower of Jesus. There are disciples who follow the teacher with total fidelity, without ever falling short. Others have troubled journeys, but they recover by drawing strength from the inexhaustible love that puts us back together again through forgiveness. Others unfortunately begin well but then get lost.

*O Jesus, help us to always believe that your love is greater than we are. It is even greater than our sins.*

Judas' despair strikes us because it is so dramatic. But there is another type of despair common today and not less dangerous. It is a bloodless kind of despair, the white despair of discouragement and insensitivity. It consists in resigning oneself to not believing, to not trying, to not committing oneself. Many call themselves non-believers or non-practicing believers only because they lack confidence or are too lazy to try. What about me?

# II. THE CIVIL TRIAL

Mt 27:1-2,11-31     Mk 15:1-20     Lk 23:1-25     Jn 18:28-40 and19:1-16

## SCENE 1: IN SEARCH OF A CRIME

**Reflect.** Another step towards death. Jesus has always considered his Passion as a handing of himself over to the forces of evil. He had been handed over to the soldiers in the garden of Gethsemane, he had been handed over to the Sanhedrin for a religious trial, and now he is handed over to the Roman authority who will hand him over to death.

According to historians, Pilate was much worse than he appears in the Gospels: cruel, arbitrary, disdainful towards the Jews. Fifth Roman governor of Judea, he held office from 26 to 36 A.D.

Jesus' trial takes place most probably in the Fortress of Antonia, near the temple, where today the Sisters of Sion reside. The procurator lived in Caesarea on the Mediterranean Sea, but during feasts he went to Jerusalem and stayed in that residence.

There is some uncertainty about the chronology. For the Synoptics Jesus is condemned and dies on Friday, the day of the Jewish Passover. For Jn, that Friday was the vigil of the Passover, which in that year would have fallen on a Saturday.

In Mt and Mk the trial begins with an interrogation. Often the evangelists omit connecting facts or other details because they presume that they are already known to their audience. Lk and Jn narrate the Roman trial in a more logical and elaborate manner. In fact, they begin with the inquiry about the accusations, which is the first step in any trial.

In Lk the entire Sanhedrin turns to Pilate to ask that Jesus be put to death, hurling all kinds of accusations against him, "We found this man perverting our nation, and forbidding us to give tribute to Caesar, and saying that he himself is the Christ, a king," 23:2.

Why these accusations? They had not come up at the examination by the Sanhedrin. What was the purpose of the religious trial if it was not taken into account? The reason is this: it is not possible to present imputations of a religious nature to a pagan political authority. But Lk does not explain this. He is interested in underlining the injustice of the trial.

The allegations are invented to condemn Jesus who is innocent. Neither Pilate nor Herod will believe the accusations, and in reality the accusers themselves do not believe them.

All three charges against Jesus could have had a foundation, but only by playing with the ambiguities. Jesus did not incite anyone in the political sense, but his message could have elated the people and filled them with enthusiasm. Jesus did not impede people from paying their taxes, but he specified giving Caesar only economic tributes, not divine. Jesus did not refuse the titles of Messiah or king, but he never intended them in a political sense.

Pilate wants the procedure to be correctly followed. Let us listen to the charges. "What accusation do you bring against this man?" Jn 18:29. Instantly, the dialogue becomes an altercation. The Jews do not want to enter the praetorium, because they do not want to become contaminated by the pagan environment, especially at this moment on the eve of the Passover. They miss no opportunity to demonstrate to Pilate that they despise him as a Roman, as a pagan and as a person. In turn, Pilate abhors them. Their reciprocal intolerance is apparent from various cues in the debate:

"If this man were not an evildoer, we would not have handed him over."

"Take him yourselves and judge him by your own law."

"It is not lawful for us to put any man to death," Jn 18:30-31.

The situation is permeated with irony. The Jews in this scenario are afraid of becoming contaminated by the pagans, but not of wanting the death of an innocent man. The criminals call the innocent a criminal. Pilate does not see clearly. The only thing which is clear is that they want Jesus dead. Pilate decides to do some investigating on his own.

**Pray.** *O Jesus, only you know the ambiguities and the deceitfulness of the human mind to justify the refusal to do good. Help me to disentangle myself from the snares of a rationality polluted by sin.*

**Promise.** The world, as long as it is subjected to sin, will always try to eliminate the values of the Gospel. I must discover the dark areas of my life and uncover the weaknesses I am ashamed of: selfishness, arrogance, resentfulness, and so forth.

## SCENE 2: THE KING OF THE JEWS

Jesus' kingship is the central issue of the civil trial. During the religious trial the evangelists clarified the messianic identity of the accused: he is the Christ, the Messiah, the Son of God, the Son of Man. During the civil trial they specify that Jesus is king.

In the Synoptics, Pilate's only question is this: "Are you the king of the Jews?" Mt 27:11. This is his main concern. The title of "king of the Jews" is new; it is used only by Pilate and hints at political power. The Jews would never call him only king, but king of Israel, the Christ, the liberator or something similar.

If Jesus really considered himself king, then Pilate would be dealing with an alarming case. It would be a threat to the imperial authority of Rome, to be immediately crushed. For this reason the astute accusers camouflaged their accusation in political terms. In the religious trial they had condemned Jesus for a religious reason—blasphemy, for calling himself the Son of God—but now they use political language.

In the Synoptics Jesus answers: "You have said so," Mk 15:2. It is the same response given to Judas during the Supper and to Caiaphas at the religious trial. It indicates that the interrogator has understood the problem but is not willing to solve it. He remains trapped in it.

There are still sparks of irony. It appears from the questions of these opponents that they grasp the truth, but are unable to accept it. This is their failure. Such is the case of Judas, of the Jewish leaders, of Pilate and of whoever in life lacks the courage to surrender to the truth.

Jesus' answer is clear and obscure at the same time. Before the Sanhedrin his answer was, "I am," Mk 14:62, because he spoke the same biblical language of his interrogators. Then, all understood that he was the Messiah and came from God. Before Pilate Jesus is more subtle: "You have said so," Mk 15:2. The meaning is: they are your words not mine; it is true, but not in the sense you intend; I accept the title, but not in your sense; you do not understand well, but my accusers do.

In Mt and Mk Jesus' answer unleashes accusations against him. The declaration is followed by a deafening uproar, so much so that Pilate prods Jesus to defend himself: "Have you no answer to make? See how many charges they bring against you," Mk 15:4. But Jesus keeps silent. He won't add another word until he is on the cross. He is like the Righteous One of Israel who remains silent in the midst of the clamor of his enemies and the abandonment of his friends, or like the Servant of God who marvels the onlookers with his strength in suffering. In fact, Pilate "was amazed," Mk 15:5.

The protagonists of the civil trial are now in the spotlight. Pilate has an initial inclination to defend Jesus, but it does not develop. The Jews, as Jn always calls them, remain sealed in their blindness. They will turn the crowd and Pilate against the Righteous One. Jesus is consistent in his fidelity to his Father and to his own mission.

The core of the conflict is Jesus' kingship. He is king but they do not understand the meaning. His kingship is love.
Every human being is involved in the trial. Myself included.

*O Jesus, help me to understand the power of your word and of your silence. Both eloquently proclaim that you are king.*

Manipulation of the identity of other people is one of the most painful distortions of human relationships. Everyone knows how wounding it is to be misunderstood or to be wrongly judged. How often do I treat others this way?

## SCENE 3: PILATE, A MISSED DISCIPLESHIP

Jn's narrative of Jesus' civil trial is a literary and theological masterpiece. The Jews are out in the square. Jesus is inside the praetorium. He is questioned and responds exhaustively. Pilate goes back and forth trying to master the situation, but in the end he will succumb to it. For a certain time he is the focal point of the scene, but then Jesus will join him and take center stage.

Jn's setting is usually divided into seven scenes, separated by Pilate's movements inside and outside.

- Outside: The Jewish leaders hand Jesus over to have him condemned.
- Inside: The first interrogation of Jesus, regarding his identity.
- Outside: Pilate's first declaration that Jesus is innocent.
- Inside: Jesus is scourged at the pillar and mocked as king of the Jews.
- Outside: Pilate's second declaration that Jesus is innocent.
- Inside: Second questioning of Jesus, regarding his origin.
- Outside: Jesus is handed over to be crucified.

Also according to Jn Pilate asks Jesus whether he is the king of the Jews. But Jesus' answer is wordier than usual and turns Pilate's arguments upside down: "Do you say this of your own accord, or did others say it to you about me?" Jn 18:34. Jesus uses Pilate's own words, but focuses their meaning and offers to explain them to his interlocutor. He begins by asking a question which leaves Pilate both curious and irritated because he is being interrogated by the one who is under interrogation.

Pilate reacts emphasizing their racial differences. It is others who are against you, not I. What is going on among you? "Am I a Jew? Your own nation and the chief priests have handed you over to me: what have you done?" 18:35.

Seeing that Pilate does not refuse to discuss the issue, Jesus speaks clearly: "My kingship is not of this world," 18:36. If it were, it would have some kind of defensive and offensive organization. This leaves Pilate even more anxious and frustrated. He pursues and insists: "So, then, you are a king?" 18:37. The one thing that worries him most is an eventual political conspiracy.

To this pagan who is trying to understand, Jesus offers a glimmer of the truth which could lead him to discipleship, as he had done earlier on with the Samaritan woman and with Nicodemus. "You say that I am a king. For this I was born and for this I have come into the world, to bear witness to the truth. Everyone who is of the truth hears my voice," 18:37.

Pilate comes close to the truth. Jesus urges him to accept it, uttering one of the most powerful Christological assertions of the Gospels.

It is as if he had said to Pilate: Stop playing hide and seek. You have understood that I am a king; now open your heart and believe the truth. I am king because I bear witness to the truth. You must understand truth in the biblical sense, not in the sense of the Greco-Roman philosophy. Truth is God, his sovereignty, his plan of salvation, his only Son sent to save the world. Truth is thus Jesus himself and all that he reveals about God and hu-

manity: the Triune God and love; the call to humanity to be friends, sons and daughters, family members and heirs of God. Truth and Jesus are the same thing. Whoever is on the side of truth recognizes and listens to him. The ultimate expression of this truth will be the cross, because there Jesus will reveal everything about God and his love.

The offer has been presented. Take it or leave it. Come on, Pilate, the truth is at hand. But he is distracted, blinded by the glare of power. He throws out a question without waiting for an answer: "What is truth?" 18:36. He is convinced that Jesus is innocent and goes outside to declare it to the people. But this is not enough. He should have become a follower of Jesus. What a pity!

*O Jesus, how many Pilates are wandering about! Many people are reluctant to resolve the problem of their relationship with Jesus only because it is demanding. Or perhaps too many of his followers, myself included, are not credible.*

Nobody can belong to Jesus without following him. Today there are too many alienating calls: interests, choices, companions, literature, spectacles, possessions. I cannot reconcile Jesus with everything. Wherever the pollution of sin is found, Jesus is always ready to forgive, but he cannot approve.

## SCENE 4: NOT GUILTY

The accusation that Jesus is a king who will threaten Caesar is a setup. It does not take long for Pilate, an expert in criminal cases, to understand this. In Mt and Mk he only resorts to an attempted exchange with Barabbas in order to free Jesus. In Jn he invents more subtle stratagems to make his judgment prevail.

First of all he openly proclaims to the Jewish leaders in a solemn statement: "I find no case against him," 18:38. A pagan maintains that Jesus is innocent while his own people consider him guilty. This detail is echoed in the failure of the first Christians in their attempt to preach the Gospel to the Jews.

Shortly Pilate will propose Barabbas as an alternative to Jesus. In the Synoptics it will be the leaders or the crowd who remind Pilate of this Passover tradition.

In Lk also Pilate affirms his conviction: "I find no case against this man," 23:4. Thus the trial could end with an acquittal. But the opponents cannot accept this, because it would mean the release of the prisoner with the equivalent of full absolution. They are infuriated by Pilate's statement and hastily hurl back the initial accusation with details regarding the geographical area: "He stirs up the people, teaching throughout all Judea, from Galilee even to this place," 23:5. This does not add much to the previous charge, but it gives them time and keeps Pilate from pronouncing the sentence of acquittal. Unfortunately, instead of coherently proceeding with the matter at hand, Pilate also takes his time.

Once again, the accusation repeated by the leaders is a mixture of falsehood and truth. The word "stir up" in Aramaic also means to divert or put on the wrong track. Jesus does not instigate either in a political or in a religious sense, but his message demands radical commitment. This may certainly imply a change in one's ways, a turn in another direction, a conversion, with all of its consequences in one's political as well as religious conduct. Therefore, this allegation can be politically exploited.

Understanding Jesus is an endless problem. It was thus for the Jews, for the Romans, for cultures throughout the centuries and even for us today. Is it possible to comprehend the kingship of love in a social or personal way of living based on selfishness and greed? How can we discern the truth that comes from God in the midst of the clamor of so many messages which bombard our daily lives and render us incapable of taking time to reflect and to listen in silence?

*O Jesus, we zigzag and wander around aimlessly in order to avoid looking truth in the face, because truth uncovers reality in all its aspects. Help me to always look to your Passion from which your truth, which is love, radiates.*

Truth is a topic that has disappeared from our conversations and concerns. It is far removed from the lifestyle to which we have reduced ourselves. But truth is essential. We cannot understand anything if we do not respect the truth which is in ourselves, in others and in all creation. I must identify the fear of truth which resides within me so that I may overcome it.

## SCENE 5: HEROD, AN UNSUCCESSFUL WAY OUT

It is not easy to avoid getting lost in the confusion of the many characters named Herod, all of them of the worst reputation. They are all Jews of Idumean origin. For some decades Rome used them to keep Palestine under control. Herod the Great was in power when Jesus was born, and ordered the massacre of the innocents. When he died in 4 A.D., his territory was divided, with the consent of the Romans, among his three sons, as cruel as he but not as intelligent.

Philip settled in the north, with Caesarea as the capital.

Antipas took Galilee and Perea, to the east of the river Jordan.

Archelaus was assigned Judea, Samaria and Idumea. He soon became so notorious that Mary and Joseph, coming back from Egypt, preferred returning to Galilee instead of settling in Judea. After only two years in power, the Romans had to get rid of him and began ruling the region through a procurator appointed by the emperor.

It is not necessary here to mention all other Herods of the same branch.

The one at the time of the Passion of Jesus is Herod Antipas. In the past he had ordered the beheading of John the Baptist and had expressed concern regarding Jesus, considered by some to be the Baptist risen from the dead.

When Pilate hears the Jews saying that the accused had worked in Galilee, he asks whether Jesus is of that region. If this is the case, Jesus is under the jurisdiction of Herod Antipas, who also is in Jerusalem for the Passover. No sooner thought than done, Pilate sends Jesus to Herod asking him to resolve this case.

Herod gladly accepts. He had heard of and wanted to meet Jesus, but he had never had the opportunity. He decides to take advantage of the situation to satisfy his curiosity and his desire to amuse himself with the miracle worker as if he were a juggler. He asks him many questions. Those keeping custody of Jesus repeat the accusations. "But he made no answer," Lk 23:9.

Lk also has in mind the Servant of God who, though overwhelmed by abuse, "opened not his mouth," Is 53:7. But silence humiliates the scornful accusers. Herod is filled with indignation; he and his attendants then ridicule him and pelt him with insults. Herod orders that Jesus be dressed in a showy robe, possibly red as a parody of his kingship or white to signify the innocence of the deranged, and taken back to Pilate.

This is the only incident of contempt against Jesus reported by Lk in the entire trial. He always tried to avoid or to attenuate descriptions of unpleasant situations.

Though annoyed by Jesus' demeanor, Herod agrees with Pilate regarding his innocence. Now that the hot potato is again in his hands, the procurator will take advantage of Herod's opinion to convince the crowd that Jesus is innocent.

With these exchanges, the two become friends once again. Perhaps because the logic of power always finds an accord at the expense of the innocent, or because with this occasion they overcame their disagreements over how to deal with the Galileans: Pilate had ordered slaughtering some of them even in the temple area.

Since Lk alone reports this appearance of Jesus before Herod, some have doubted its historical basis. Perhaps the other inspired authors were unaware of this detail or did not consider it relevant to convey any special lesson. None of the evangelists tells everything, but each selects words and facts according to the message he intends to transmit to the recipient communities. Lk uses the occurrence to signal Pilate's wavering mood, always searching for a way to escape instead of following his conscience. The evangelist also intends to denounce the wrong way of being concerned about Jesus, based only on curiosity.

*O my Jesus, you keep on affirming your identity and dignity, to Pilate with words and to Herod with silence. Help me not to be conditioned either by acceptance or by rejection in my fidelity to you and to the Gospel.*

Pilate and Herod represent two erroneous ways of solving the Jesus-problem: the first by trying to unload it, the second by making light of it. The only correct way is by following Jesus. I must verify that this is my way.

## Scene 6: The exchange with a criminal

Barabbas appears in all four Gospels. No other historical source mentions this individual, but the Gospels are more than sufficient. Freeing a prisoner for the Passover was possibly a tacit concession by the Romans, of great significance to the Jews: it was a reminder of their liberation from Egypt and from other forms of slavery in their history.

In Mt and Mk Barabbas' name surfaces soon after Pilate's question on kingship. In Jn, after the first, and in Lk, after the second declaration of innocence. For Mt the comparison between Jesus and Barabbas is the central element in the trial.

Here is the way the scene unfolds according to Mt and Mk. The members of the Sanhedrin are arguing with Pilate to convince him to condemn Jesus. The crowd is not present yet because the people have not yet been informed about what is happening. At a certain point in the morning, many people gather for the annual appointment with the Roman governor who will propose the freeing of a prisoner. The leaders take advantage of this turnout to convince those present to call for the liberation of Barabbas and the death sentence for Jesus.

Some ancient sources maintain that Barabbas also was named Jesus. In fact, Pilate's words may have been: Do you want me to free for you Jesus who is called "Barabbas or Jesus who is called Christ?" Mt 27:17. Since Barabbas means "son of the Father" and Jesus calls himself "Son of God," the comparison is striking.

Jn remarks that Barabbas is a robber. Mt calls him a notorious prisoner. Mk and Lk inform us that with his gang he committed murder in an insurrection. He probably belongs to the movement of the zealots, a group of nationalists or terrorists who lost no occasion to express their discontent with Roman rule. Two others will be executed with Jesus.

Mt offers a further elaboration, showing us Pilate who is anguished by an unexpected intervention from his wife. She had nightmares about the consequences of this trial. This detail magnifies the contrast: the Jewish people, though nurtured by revelation since the beginning of their history, now reject the promised and awaited-for Messiah; the pagans, who never knew revelation, are disturbed by a mysterious warning from on high.

Pilate expected the comparison with Barabbas would turn out in favor of Jesus. Mk's formulation of the question shows his attempt to suggest a positive answer: "Do you want me to release for you the king of the Jews?" 15:9. Pilate, however, knew that "it was out of envy that the chief priests had delivered him up," 15:10, the same envy that had induced the devil to introduce sin into the world, Ws 2:24.

But in little time the crowd is manipulated. Until now it supported Jesus, but at this point it joins the opposition, together with Judas and the Sanhedrin. The answer is a shout that comes in three waves: "Barabbas! Barabbas! Barabbas!"

When Pilate angrily asks about the fate of Jesus, the chorus of voices urges: "Crucify him! Crucify him!" Mk 15:13,14.

Since Pilate refuses to assume responsibility, they take it

on themselves: "His blood be on us and on our children!" Mt 27:25.

By washing his hands, Pilate makes a choice though pretending not to choose. The Jewish leaders and the crowd spurn the covenant which was the backbone of their history. They all take the same side: the rejection of the truth. To encounter Jesus implies choosing: to accept or to reject him. By rejecting, one takes sides with the opposition, goes against the truth and pronounces one's own sentence of condemnation, which even God is bound to respect.

*O Jesus, help me to choose you, along with all that comes from you and leads to you.*

In our life everything comes down to choosing and being chosen. I must examine which of my choices are in accordance with Jesus Christ and which ones are not. I must also identify those occasions when in practice I choose Barabbas because I fail to decidedly choose Jesus.

SCENE 7: I REPEAT: NOT GUILTY

The outcry of the mob still rings in Pilate's ears. He had prepared the trap and now finds himself caught in it. As a result, the way out is much more complicated. If he had not reduced the case to an alternative, it would have been possible to continue the trial by debating the pros and cons. But now the proceedings are blocked. Having lost the possibility of freeing Jesus, Pilate has no choice but to condemn an innocent man.

He does not give up. Even in Mk, whose narrative is faster paced and the opposition less virulent, Pilate tries to postpone a decision: "Then what should I do with this man whom you call the king of the Jews?" Mk 15:12. It is a useless question but it expresses the spitefulness of the procurator. The answer unfolds the purpose of Mk's account: to attain the full revelation of Jesus' identity on the cross.

Mt's report shows that Pilate is incapable of being consistent though stubborn in his conviction. He washes his hands to proclaim his own innocence instead of defending the innocence of the Innocent. However, it is impossible to evade responsibilities with words or theatrical gestures.

In Lk Pilate had summoned all the concerned parties, almost like a national and universal assembly, to proclaim Jesus' innocence after he returned from Herod: "Pilate then called together the chief priests and the rulers and the people, and said to them: 'You brought me this man as one who was misleading the people; and, behold, after interrogating him in your presence, I have not found this man guilty of any of your charges against him; moreover, neither has Herod, for he sent him back to us. Behold, he has done nothing deserving of death,'" 23:13-15.

Lk does not have a weak spot for Pilate, but he makes it clear that during the trial he is the only one to defend Jesus with declarations of legal value. Pilate and Herod are the two legal witnesses to prove Jesus' righteousness. Four times in a few verses he affirms that he finds no fault in Jesus—three times before and one time after the crowd chooses Barabbas, 23:4, 14, 15, 22. In the end, overwhelmed by the violent reactions of Jesus' enemies he gives in, likewise swallowed up by the darkness.

Lk accentuates both Jesus' unimpeachability and the Jews' tenaciousness in repudiating him. Moreover, Lk intends to guarantee to the Roman authorities that Christians are not resentful towards them, and that they are not revolutionaries, just as Jesus was not. They appreciate the efforts made by their representative in favor of Jesus.

In Jn, Pilate pretends not to take into account the fact that the crowd chose Barabbas. His imagination resorts to new expedients. Since the attempted exchange with the murderer failed, he comes up with the scourging. Having lost by appealing to rationality, he hopes to prevail by appealing to the emotions. He carefully prepares a scene of great spectacular effect, capable even of melting rocks: the flagellation.

The exhausting tug of war in this trial shows that the evangelists consider it of paramount importance. It is the decisive moment: the acceptance or the rejection of the Savior.

Pilate is determined to free Jesus. He reiterates it both in words and by inventing unexpected ways of escape. The Jews want him dead. They called him an "evildoer," Jn 18:30, and then chose an evildoer instead of him. Evildoers always choose one of their own.

Logic, consistency, faithfulness to truth and to oneself, human dignity itself, all vanish in this trial. Only Jesus personifies and defends these values.

*O my Jesus, we see the human comedy run its course shamelessly during the religious and civil trials against you. Without God it is impossible to be a fully decent human being. Sin, which is delusion and division, ruins everything.*

In a certain sense, human life is an ongoing trial. We are always exposed to others and subjected to their judgment. In turn, we do the same to them. It is impossible to avoid compromise and manipulation. The only solution is to link everything to truth in love, as Jesus did. This must always be my rule of life.

## SCENE 8: THE SCOURGING

The evangelists mention it but not one of them describes it.

Lk does not speak of it because it is unbecoming of his presentation of Jesus. We can imagine it through the words Pilate uses to satisfy Jesus' adversaries: "I will chastise him and release him," Lk 23:16.

Mt and Mk link the scourging to the death sentence, as was the custom. Pilate "having scourged Jesus, delivered him to be crucified," Mt 27:26. The one who was to be crucified was routinely scourged to prepare the body for the nailing. The pain was attenuated and death accelerated.

Jn places the scourging at the center of the trial as a means through which Pilate appeals to the emotions of the people, to extract from them the consent to liberate Jesus.

After the people unexpectedly chose the liberation of Barabbas, Pilate retreats into the praetorium, leaving the crowd and the leaders in suspense. The pause may have lasted more than an hour since the scourging was followed by a mockery of Jesus. The delay increases the emotional tension.

"Pilate took Jesus and scourged him," 19:1.

Meditation on the Passion has always given great importance to the scourging, notwithstanding the fact that the evangelists do not concern themselves with the physical suffering of Jesus. A mystery of the Rosary is dedicated to the scourging at the pillar.

Flogging caused unbearable pain. Jewish law restricted this chastisement to forty lashes, but for the Romans there was no limit. It was left up to those who administered the scourging and depended on the resistance of the condemned.

The scourge consisted of strips of leather or of a bunch of cords which may have had pieces of iron or bone at the tips to tear the flesh. One could even die from the brutality of these blows. The Romans only inflicted this punishment on slaves and foreigners.

Today, when we see or read about children who have been abused or people who have been tortured during conflicts, we recoil in disgust. And yet human beings have treated one other in this way for centuries, even for pleasure and entertainment. These sufferings have been shared also by Jesus.

In Gethsemane Jesus experienced our anguish and our solitude. In the trials he endured the misunderstandings and exploitations that are often part and parcel of our human condition. In the scourging he participates in the suffering to which the human body may be subjected. Our body is a work of God, but because of sin it is subject to every imaginable kind of grief and pain: illness, surgery, armed conflict which maims, burns or asphyxiates, rape, mayhem, the gas chambers.

We are horrified by the ancient practice of scourging, yet the progress of civilization has simply refined ways to flog the human body. Many afflictions of the human body derive from the abuse of its positive functions: sexual activity, eating, working, having fun.

Handed over to the power of darkness, that is to the power of sin, Jesus accepts upon his own body the consequences of sin, among which violence is the first.

His silence speaks of love, dignity, and endurance, but it also denounces violence and abuse of the body.

We must not forget that the scourging also entails moral pain, since it is another sign of rejection on the part of those who willed it.

*O Jesus, your scourging sends shivers of horror through our bodies and moves our emotions. May I remain close to you when suffering seizes me, and close to others when suffering seizes them.*

In times of pain and hardship, I must remember Jesus' silence and love during the scourging to find meaning in difficult situations. I must realize that my body is a gift that I have received and that I am to use it in the service of others within my family and at work. My body should be the musical instrument of my soul.

## SCENE 9: MOCKING THE KING

The scourging is followed by a parody of a regal coronation and homage to a king. In Jn it is described briefly because its purpose is to prepare the subsequent scene of the Ecce Homo. "The soldiers wove a crown of thorns and placed it on his head, and put a purple robe on him; they came up to him, saying: 'Hail, king of the Jews!' And struck him with their hands," 19:2-3. The passage clearly expresses the irony which is at the core of the trial.

In Mt and Mk the depiction is more expressive of the fact

that Jesus is rejected here in his identity as a king. Just as after the religious trial the mockery indicated his rejection as the Messiah, so after the civil trial the regal parody expresses his rejection as a king, no matter how his kingship might be interpreted.

The mockery of a convict was quite common, but the evangelists load it with theological significance. The soldiers who had in their custody the prisoners who were condemned to death often amused themselves by insulting them and playing cruel jokes on them. In Jesus' case the entire cohort, that is six hundred soldiers, is said to have taken part.

The spectacle consists of two phases, each with three actions.

*First phase, parody of the regal vestments.*

1. The soldiers strip Jesus of his garments and put a scarlet cloak on him, the kind used by the Roman soldiers. Both Jn and Mk say "purple," to allude to kingship.
2. On his head they put a crown of thorns taken from the firewood or from the thickets growing in the area.
3. They put a reed in his hand.

A cloak, a crown and a scepter are the insignia of kingship.

*Second phase, parody of royal homage.*

1. They kneel before him and sarcastically laugh: "Hail, king of the Jews."
2. They spit upon him.
3. They take the reed from his hand and beat the crown of thorns into his head.

It is the outrageous and villainous caricature of the homage due to a king. Its violence leaves us disconcerted. The abuse of a prisoner stains humanity nowadays also. Jesus finds himself in the middle of wickedness personified.

The paradox is that their parody proclaims and demonstrates the reality. They affirm what they deny. They mock the king to prove that he is not a king, but in so doing they give him the opportunity to show that he is king as he intends.

Once again the irony of the situation fairly explodes. According to his opponents the paradox lies in the fact that Jesus claims to be a king while he is not. In reality, however, Jesus is king and they unknowingly confirm it. His kingdom is not of this world.

The kingship of love manifests itself when a person is rejected, beaten, spat upon, and yet continues to love. Jesus' power consists of giving his own life, a body broken and blood poured for the salvation of the world. It will be revealed fully on the cross, but its manifestation is already in progress. He will reign from the cross, but he already reigns from the praetorium, among the insults of rejection. The event of Calvary will be similar to this: a lifting up and a rejection. Everything now gravitates towards the cross, where the identity of Jesus and of the disciple will appear in all its clarity.

Thus the Gospels convey the theological meaning of the Passion, whereas its sorrowful aspects have prevailed down through the centuries in meditations on the Passion. Both are important but must be integrated.

The abundance of Gospel details on this point accentuates the tragedy of rejecting Jesus. He is repudiated by all: the leaders, the masses, the Jews, and the Romans, each as they understand him. Yet he continues to love all of them. This is true kingship. Rejection turns against itself and becomes the loudest proclamation of the truth. No affirmation was ever stronger than this denial.

*O my Jesus, sin and its consequences in human life cry out that your love is stronger than all and never fails. It is the truth that resists every attack. It is the truth that judges our life's success or failure.*

I must be able to identify where Jesus is scorned or denied today. It may happen around me, among the people with whom

I associate and even in my family. I also may be among those who continue to insult him if I fail to respect and defend the dignity of every human being.

## SCENE 10: BEHOLD THE MAN

Pilate, the skilled actor, once again takes control of the situation. He takes advantage of the scourging and of the royal parody for an ideological and spectacular purpose. This is why he ordered the flagellation and permitted the mockery to take place. Perhaps Pilate also intends to give an exhibition of his own power, since Jesus is speaking of another mysterious power.

The crowd is still waiting outside, mumbling over the delay. Pilate theatrically appears on the balcony and proclaims in a challenging tone: "Behold I am bringing him out to you, so that you may know that I find no case against him," 19:4. And soon Jesus appears on stage "wearing the crown of thorns and the purple robe." Pointing to him Pilate rhetorically says: "Behold the man," 19:5.

How is it possible to have reduced him to this state if he is innocent?

A chilling silence follows.

Pilate believes he has been successful. He has played the winning card. If they insist on wanting him dead they are inhuman, worse than hungry savage beasts before their prey.

This is another central scene of the Passion. It has inspired artists, ignited mystics with love, and touched the hearts of fervent as well as lukewarm Christians.

What does Pilate mean by this sentence? Does he mean "the man" we were dealing with? Or is he echoing the title "Son of Man," so preferred by the Synoptics? The latter cannot be excluded.

We could dwell on this scene for a long time, fixing our eyes and our heart on it. Jesus watches the crowd while everyone watches him. He gazes intently at the people and at humanity. His eyes read the souls of all, to our days and beyond, including you and me. He is *the* Human Being, reduced by sin and elevated by God. He is torn and disfigured, but still able to love and to forgive.

But Pilate's move fails. The high priests and the guards shout all the louder: "Crucify him! Crucify him!"

Pilate wildly insists on throwing back an improbable option: "Take him yourselves and crucify him, for I find no case against him," 19:6.

Until now the Jews have not accused Jesus of anything before Pilate. They have introduced him as an evildoer, have preferred Barabbas to him, yet nothing serious has emerged against him. Now they throw the religious accusation against him: "We have a law, and by that law he deserves to die, because he has made himself the Son of God," 19:7.

It is the crime of blasphemy, for which at least three times, in Jn, the Jews attempted to stone Jesus, 5:18; 8:59; 10:31-39. It is the same violation which surfaced during the religious trial. The fundamental titles of Jesus' identity reappear again. Pilate reminds them that Jesus is *the man*, that is, the Son of Man with divine traits. The Jews remind Pilate that Jesus said he is the Son of God. "When Pilate heard these words, he became more afraid than ever," 19:8. He realizes that he has taken things too lightly. He feels as if he must begin again.

*O my Jesus, you are the Man, the human being loaded with all the weaknesses of humanity, but called to journey toward salvation. You represent the human being facing his responsibilities before God and his neighbors. You are the human being who represents me also.*

Big mistakes in life come from smaller ones. Pilate slowly slips down the slope of compromise: he does not listen to the word of Jesus when he begins revealing himself; he sends Jesus to Herod; he compares him to Barabbas the murderer; he has

Jesus scourged only to prepare an emotional exhibition. His last tragic mistake will be to condemn Jesus to death. I must always stop myself after the first mistake and then resume my journey.

SCENE 11: LOOKING AT THE MAN

The scene of the Ecce Homo is as important as that of the cross. In it Jn, Mt and Mk condense, as in an indelible snapshot, the crowning of thorns and the royal parody. Jn, in particular, gives the impression that he wants to dwell on the scene instead of hastily skimming over it. He stops it and magnifies it so that everyone can look at the Man, just as he will later quote the Scriptures which invite everyone to "look on him whom they have pierced," 19:37.

The man camouflaged as a king is Jesus, but he represents humanity in general, often clothed in superficial values that ridicule and make a fool of the person. God created human beings to be kings, the noblest creatures of the universe, the link between God and the cosmos; however man broke the tie with God, and can no longer be lord of creation. On the contrary, he is often subjected to it. Wanting to dominate without God, he became slave to the things over which he should have dominion.

Jesus is robed with the accessories of fake kingship: the crown of thorns, the red cloak, the reed in his hand, and the blood from his wounds. He receives fake homage: bows, genuflections, spits, sneers and blows with the reed. Everything that is usually a sign of glory becomes a sign of humiliation.

He is like modern man in the midst of realities over which he should have dominion. His studies and his knowledge should bring him closer to God and make him respectful of creation; instead, he pulls himself away from God and decimates nature. Progress and material well-being should render him more fraternal and thankful; instead, he becomes more and more selfish, arrogant, greedy and uncaring towards the less fortunate.

God alone is the ultimate and absolute value. All other values take second place and are relative. The latter, positive in themselves, can be the sign of human kingship if they are subordinate to God; but they become the sign of man's defeat if they are considered absolute. This happens when the body and its expressions like sex, talent, beauty, health, and leisure, and when material goods like money, success, power, cultural prestige and social savoir-faire become supreme goals for which everything else is sacrificed, even the soul.

The Man-Jesus became a mock king so that every human being might cease being mocked by the realities over which he or she should be lord.

As in the flagellation Jesus wanted to redeem the abuse of the human body and at the same time share and give value to its sufferings, in the crowning of thorns he redeems the flaws and abuse of the human mind. In the symbolism of our language the head is the source of thought. From it flows all good and all evil planned and put into action by humanity. In his silent pain Jesus assumes and gives value to the good and he ransoms and purifies the evil that flows from the human mind.

*O Jesus, do not allow me to be dominated by those realities I am called to guide according to the plan of creation and salvation. Help me to contribute to nature's harmony and to people's fulfillment.*

I must realize that intelligence is a gift to be developed and used according to God's will. Whatever I may desire or plan for my own happiness is always less than what God desires and plans for me. I must try to be subject to his will by meditating on the Bible and the teachings of the Church. Prayer and meditation on the Passion will help me build my life in union with the will of God.

## SCENE 12: AN ADDITIONAL INQUIRY

"Behold the man," Pilate said to the people. "Behold God," the crowd replied. "He claims to be the Son of God." Pilate's fear grows. He decides to resume his dialogue with Jesus.

In a previous conversation he had tried to determine Jesus' identity and remained entangled by his responses: a kingdom which is not of this world, the truth, et cetera. Perhaps Pilate's fear comes also from this mysterious talk.

It is even more difficult now to speak with a prisoner reduced to such a state. Maybe it is not possible to look him in
the eyes, and his face must be like a smeared mask.

Will they be able to understand each other? How does one
find common ground between such different worlds? It is enough
to look at their faces. There is a painting that presents them face
to face, Pilate wearing a crown of laurel and Jesus wearing a
crown of thorns. It is obvious that they cannot communicate.
The head of the former is filled with concerns over power. The
demeanor of the latter expresses the majesty of love that over-
comes rejection, while he is determined to do the will of the
Father and to witness to the truth.

This time Pilate starts the inquiry with the origin of the
interlocutor: "Where are you from? You will not speak to me?
Do you not know that I have power to release you, and power
to crucify you?" Jn 19:9-10.

Jesus realizes that Pilate is by now closed to faith; therefore, at first he does not answer. Then, to curb Pilate's boasting
about his power, he points out: "You would have no power over
me unless it had been given you from above; therefore he who
delivered me to you has the greater sin," Jn 19:11.

He continues to speak. Unlike the Jesus of the Synoptics,
Jn's Jesus talks like an orator. He defends himself from manipulation in the political sense. Now he recognizes Pilate's power,
but defines its limits. Yes, he can judge Jesus, but by a power
from on high, given for this special case, because the plan of salvation must be carried out.

Pilate has power over Jesus only because Jesus chose to give
his life out of love for the salvation of the world. The issue here
is not that every authority comes from God, cf. Rm 13:1-2. This
principle is true only so long as that authority is exercised according to the will of God. The abuse of power is not from God,
and it is not God's intention to approve it.

The same mystery we encountered in Judas' betrayal
emerges here. Only God guides Jesus' destiny. Jesus is going to
die, not because the plot against him has succeeded or because

Pilate will condemn him to death, but because he has the power
to give up his life out of love. But around this drama all act according to their own responsibilities. As a matter of fact, there
is a "greater sin." Perhaps Jesus alludes to the sin of Judas or to
that of the Sanhedrin.

Pilate's second interrogation of Jesus ends like the first. He
does not understand his reasoning, but is even more convinced
of his innocence. He reappears before the crowd still determined
to defend his opinion against everyone.

*O Jesus, the exercise of authority can give way to conflict within family, society and church. Help me to live it in the light of faith—to accept it with humility and to practice it as a service.*

At times, faith is reduced to something like an expired license or a dead battery. It is there but it does not work. You realize this when you need faith to face a difficult situation such as an illness, a misunderstanding, or a death: you resort to it but it does not help you. Meditation on the Passion recharges life with faith. I confirm my determination to continue meditating upon it.

## SCENE 13: HERE IS YOUR KING

Pilate tries desperately to succeed, but the obstinacy of the Jews prevails. Since the procurator insists that Jesus is innocent after he had heard the charges of a religious nature, the Jews quickly launch a political accusation against Jesus: "If you release this man, you are no 'Friend of Caesar'; everyone who makes himself a king sets himself against Caesar," 19:12.

They, the Jews, pretend to be Caesar's friends and insinuate that Pilate, the Roman representative of the emperor, is an enemy. This is a clear threat—they will take the case to Rome.

Pilate realizes he has fallen into the trap. He will not be able to avoid condemning Jesus to death even though he is still convinced of his innocence. This is the power he boasts about? It cannot even protect the innocent. Annoyed and resentful, he brings Jesus out and moves to the final phase of the trial.

"He led Jesus outside and sat down on the judgment seat," 19:13. Some scholars think that the verb "sat down" should be translated transitively, therefore the sentence should read as follows: Pilate led Jesus outside and "sat him down" on the judge's seat. A few national liturgical lectionaries have adopted this translation. If this were the case, the scene could have made a disconcerting impression.

However, nothing changes. Pilate proclaims: "Here is your king," 19:14. Another crucial moment has arrived. His words are both a proclamation and a legal sentence. Jn underlines the strict link with the Passover: "It was the day of preparation for the Passover; it was about noon," the same hour when the pascal lambs were slaughtered. In Jn the entire civil trial is an affirmation of Jesus' kingship. This is its climax.

The answer is a loud shout: "Away with him, away with him! Crucify him!" Pilate retorts: "Shall I crucify your king?" 19:15.

The struggle between defense and prosecution is at its highest. Pilate keeps on using royal terminology. Instead of condemning Jesus, he proclaims him king. Clearly, he is unable to overcome the pressure of the Jews, but he is also incapable of proclaiming an innocent person guilty. In fact, he does not pronounce a death sentence. Or, if you like, he condemns Jesus with a sentence which is at the same time a royal proclamation. His last words are: your king.

The sacrilegious rejection thunders from the courtyard: "We have no king but Caesar," 19:15. Some scholars doubt the historical truth of this sentence. It seems impossible that Jews of that time and in that political situation could have prostituted themselves to the Roman emperor to this point. They condemn a fellow citizen because of blasphemy and now they themselves utter the most incredible blasphemy that is at the same time an apostasy from God their king. The people of God, bound to God by the covenant, having no other king but God, now scream that they have no king but Caesar.

Jn could not have chosen a more effective setting to express the crazed rejection of the Savior. Jesus, whether standing or seated in the tribunal, is judged while judging the world.

*O Jesus, I am happy to proclaim you my king. I adore and love you as the only king of my life and of the world.*

I must not be scandalized by the wretchedness into which

the human condition may precipitate. Instead I should be pre-occupied about mediocrity in my own spiritual life. Lukewarmness is very dangerous and may be a foreboding of a turning away from faith and from Jesus Christ.

## SCENE 14: HANDED OVER TO BE CRUCIFIED

No death was ever anticipated as this one. Jesus' predictions of being handed over, condemned and executed abound in the Gospels. The turning point before the final stretch is the Roman trial.

After Jn, Mt offers the most elaborate account of it. He dramatically accentuates the rupture caused by the rejection of Jesus. He gives importance to the choosing of Barabbas and to the paradox that two pagans, Pilate and his wife, defend Jesus while his own people demand that he be condemned. It should be emphasized that Mt's account of the Jewish rejection of Jesus has strong polemical elements, and cannot be taken as evidence that the Jews are guilty of deicide.

In Mt's account, God was faithful to his promise and sent a Savior, but his people rejected him. Now the offer is passed to a new people. This echoes the expulsion of the Christian community from the synagogue by the Pharisaical Jews at the end of the first century and is, at the same time, a warning to the Christian community: those considered outsiders may be closer to them than some so-called insiders.

Pilate, to avoid a riot, then hands Jesus over to the soldiers to be crucified.

Mk expresses this in very few lines. Everything happens swiftly, in sudden fits and starts: question, answer, Jesus' silence, choosing of Barabbas, death sentence, cross. Pilate is certain about Jesus' innocence but he is not able to set him free. He soon gives in for fear of complications. Rejected by all—the Jewish and Roman leaders, the people and even his disciples—Jesus is left with no support: "So Pilate, wishing to satisfy the crowd, released Barabbas to them; and after having Jesus scourged he handed him over to be crucified," 15:15.

Lk attenuates everyone's failures and accentuates Jesus' splendid success. The master cannot be abandoned by all, because the relationship between the teacher and the disciple must be maintained.

There are no brutal lashes in Lk. He softens the comparison between Barabbas and Jesus, skips the description of the royal parody, stresses Pilate's agitation to assert Jesus' integrity.

Jesus' righteousness, however, is not Pilate's merit. He speaks much but accomplishes little, therefore he is just as responsible as the others for rejecting Jesus.

Lk does not even dare name the cross. "Pilate decided that their demand should be carried out. So he released the one they were asking for... while Jesus he handed over to their will," 23:24-25. The two contrasting poles are the innocence of Jesus and the enormity of their rejection of him.

Jn's rich narrative has accompanied us through the maze of the mystery, thanks to Jesus' participation in the trial. A curious and anxious Pilate interrogates Jesus. Jesus responds with the usual eloquence of the fourth Gospel. Often it is not clear who is on trial, Jesus or Pilate. It is not Jesus who is afraid, nervous or insecure, but Pilate. It is he who is challenged to side with the truth. He is invited to understand that his power is important but comes from on high and implies responsibility and service, not arbitrary use.

Jn's narrative offers the best presentation of Pilate. He makes both correct and incorrect decisions. He does not have the greater fault but at the same time he fails to do what is essential: to risk all for the truth. He is successful in obtaining from the Jews an improbable declaration of subjection to Caesar, but not in being consistent with his own conscience. "He handed him over to them to be crucified," 19:16.

Jesus stands out at the center of the tribunal. The universal rejection falls on him, but does not sweep him away. He is the Man, the King, the Truth, therefore, also the Judge. No rejection of truth can destroy truth. He who refuses it condemns himself, especially because he refuses love.

*O Jesus, may I never exclude you from my life. Help me to adhere to the values that have their source in you.*

The unjust condemnation of Jesus is shocking, but the absurdity of condemning and exterminating others today has reached gigantic proportions. Stalin is responsible for thirty million deaths, Hitler for about twenty, Lenin for about ten, the Chinese leaders for about thirty. People have been killed solely because of differences in race or ideology. I must learn to understand history in the light of Jesus' Passion.

SCENE 15: THE SHIPWRECK OF THE ARK

The Gospel narratives of Jesus' trial contain obvious anti-Semitic elements, which throughout the centuries were the pretext for non-Christian behavior among Christians. The most embarrassing references are found in Mt and Jn, while Mk and Lk are less compliant with such an interpretation.

Instead of engaging in tortuous reasoning to find excuses for these elements it is better to honestly admit them. The rejection of Jesus by the leaders and the crowd is unquestionable in all the Passion narratives. Let us look once again at the two most delicate points at issue.

The first is in Mt 27:25: "All the people answered: 'His blood be on us and on our children.'" It means that, in the event that Jesus is innocent, the responsibility of his death falls on those who utter his condemnation and on their descendants.

An attenuation of Mt's stance may derive from the following theological considerations: Jesus personally chose to give up his life for the salvation of the world; since he died for our sins, all of humanity is responsible for his death. In any case, the Church has rejected the idea of a perpetual curse on the Jews deriving from this passage.

The second is in Jn 19:15: "We have no king but Caesar." The remark is contrary to the entire revelation of the Old Testament, continually affirming that God is the sole king of Israel. The implication in Jn is that this involves the Jewish leaders in idolatry, since the Roman emperor claimed divine attributes for himself and required that the people recognize them.

A Roman authority, Pontius Pilate, affirms that Jesus is the king of the Jews. He proclaims the truth, although he does not fully understand its significance. The high priests, guardians of the covenant and mediators between God and his people, reject the Son of God and submit themselves to the rule of Caesar.

In both cases it is a matter of a unilateral severing of the covenant by the leaders of the chosen people. A new covenant begins with Jesus, whose purpose is to gather a new people from all nations.

It is painful to admit that a Gospel like Jn's, so rich with Jesus' lessons on unity, has become a pretext for a bitter division between Jews and Christians.

The anti-Semitism of Mt can be explained by comparing his community and the reorganization of the synagogue after 70 A.D. The first Christians thought that the rejection of Jesus by the Jews following his resurrection was no less blameworthy than the previous one.

In Jn, the anti-Semitism can be explained as a reaction to the persecutions of the synagogue against the Christians at the end of the first century. A Jewish prayer of that time said more or less: cursed be all renegade Jews, the followers of Jesus included.

During the persecution of the Christians in Rome, the Jews were tolerated, but those who were expelled from the synagogue for becoming Christians could have been pointed out to the

Roman authorities and so risked severe condemnation and even death.

These situations, which find an echo in the Gospels, nursed a certain resentment on the part of Christians towards the "perfidious Jews," to the point that figures like St. Augustine of Hippo and St. Thomas Aquinas justified hatred of them because of their responsibility for Jesus' death.

We can somehow understand this initial anti-Semitic backlash, even though it is unjustifiable. Not all Jews of all times can be considered responsible for the death of Jesus, but only certain members of the Sanhedrin of his time who were not unanimous in their decision, and the crowd present that day in the square of the praetorium. Jesus, Mary, the apostles and the first Christian communities were all Jews.

In today's ecumenical spirit, many scholars are rethinking the role of the Jewish people in the history of salvation, suggesting that their covenant did not end with Jesus' mission on earth. We must appreciate them and include them in our fraternal charity. They are our "elder brothers" in faith.

*O my Jesus, your Passion is for all, as is your love. Belonging to you makes us all equal and every other belonging becomes secondary.*

Racist language and attitudes continue to pollute the lives of Christians, not only towards Jews, but also with reference to other forms of legitimate diversity. I must examine if there are traces of such racism in my life, and uproot them in the name of the unifying love of the crucified Jesus.

# Act IV

# Calvary

# I. THE WAY

Mt 27:32      Mk 15:21-22      Lk 23:26-32      Jn 19:17

## Scene 1: Carrying Jesus' cross

**Reflect.** The Synoptics attest to the fact that someone helps Jesus carry the cross on the way to Calvary. It is a Jew of the Diaspora, that is, someone residing outside of his homeland. He comes from Cyrene, a Greek city which was the capital of Cyrenaica, a region on the coast of Libya in North Africa. His name is Simon. His family must have been well-known by Mk's community, because the evangelist specifies that he is "the father of Alexander and Rufus," 15:21. He is returning from the fields where he has been to visit his land or to settle some business affairs before the Passover begins.

According to Mt and Mk he is spotted by the soldiers and "compelled" to carry the cross of Jesus. The Greek word used is of Persian origin and indicates to be forced to do something without recompense. Perhaps he appeared to be in good physical condition. He is required to carry the crossbeam, that is the horizontal part of the cross. In a certain sense it is more arduous to carry it than the entire cross, because it is unsteady on the shoulders. The soldiers used to tie it to the outstretched arms of the condemned. The vertical pole is already planted in the ground on Golgotha.

Lk makes no mention of Simon's being "compelled." According to him it was possible that the Cyrenean spontaneously offered to help Jesus. Of the three that were to be executed, Jesus is clearly the weakest. "They laid the cross on him, to carry it behind Jesus," 23:26.

The wording calls to mind the language of following Jesus used by Lk. In Lk 9:23 Jesus had said: "If anyone would come after me, let him deny himself and take up his cross daily and follow me." And in 14:27: "Whoever does not bear his own cross and come after me, cannot be my disciple."

Mt and Mk insinuate that the cross must be carried. Often we do not like it, but there is no way out; this is why we need a push or someone who forces us to carry it, giving the impression of being compelled.

Lk reminds us that the disciple readily carries Jesus' cross, which is daily life, without being forced and without expecting or looking for sensational crosses.

As long as we do so in a positive sense, we can call a cross all of the burdens which life asks us to shoulder. Physical burdens: from our school books to grocery bags, from the work of our hands to the fatigue associated with our social and church responsibilities. Moral and physical burdens: relationships among family members, friends and in society; illnesses of our minds and bodies throughout life. To live a Christian life means to accept and embrace all this while following and imitating Jesus.

Through the episode of the Cyrenean the evangelists point to the importance of sharing the crosses of today's crucified. This man who appears and disappears in a mere biblical verse has become the symbol of all of Jesus' followers. Forced or voluntarily, he carries the cross of another. This other is Jesus. He exemplifies altruism and Christian charity at its best. When you strip yourself of egoism, to go out of your way to help another, you help Jesus carry the cross.

**Pray.** *O my Jesus, may I never feel compelled to carry the cross. May I always understand its meaning, live it and manifest it to the world.*

**Promise.** Jesus' Passion continues on all levels of human life. On a societal level, the twentieth century has been a painful station of the way of the cross. Two world wars and wars of ideologies have resulted in more than eighty million innocent deaths. Civil and ethnic wars have produced more deaths than nuclear war. This is the passion of our brothers and sisters, and thus it is the Passion of Jesus. How do I help carry these crosses? What is my reaction when I read or listen to the media reports?

## SCENE 2: A CROWD FOLLOWS JESUS

A throng of people goes to Calvary for Jesus' crucifixion. We all walk this road when we make the way of the cross, but it may happen that we miss some of its implications.

Lk, faithful to his narrative approach, underlines the fact that not all are against Jesus. At the moment of departure, it seems that the entire Sanhedrin furiously drags Jesus to Calvary. Pilate "delivered Jesus up to their will," and they "led him away," 23:25-26.

Who is the subject of these actions? They appear to be the same ones who had come from the Sanhedrin and had taken him to Pilate. Historically this is improbable, but stylistically it is very effective, for it expresses the unrelenting rejection which continues to pursue Jesus even after he is condemned—to Calvary, to the cross and to his death.

"They also led away two other criminals with him to be killed," 23:32. Each condemned person was placed in the custody of four soldiers, armed with spears and whips, who carried out the execution.

Who else could have been part of this ominous group of concerned persons? Probably friends, relatives, women from Galilee, the curious, some sadists who enjoyed seeing others suffer, those who in the square yelled, "Crucify him!"

Lk informs us that "a large crowd of people was following him, as well as some women who were bewailing and lamenting him," 23:27. Just a short time earlier, in the last stages of the Roman trial, it seemed that the entire crowd was against

Jesus. But on the way of the cross and by the cross itself there is a crowd that "follows" Jesus and is on his side.

Lk, once again, touches on the theme of following Jesus. There are a number of people, neither disciples nor friends, interested in Jesus' fate. They are struck by his suffering and by the way in which he endures it. The trip to Calvary has affected them. In the end the heart of these people will be transformed. The event of Calvary will demonstrate that many had followed Jesus. Even today when we read Lk, we feel involved.

From the twelfth century, perhaps favored by the crusades, the practice of the Way of the Cross has been widespread within the Church. Some of the stations are not found in the Gospels, but this does not mean that they are not true. Perhaps at that moment the evangelists did not have special messages to transmit. Not everything that Jesus said and did has been handed down to us.

The falls during the journey were frequent, because streets were rough and the condemned were exhausted, as was the case for Jesus. One version of the Way of the Cross from 1490 lists seven falls. Friends tried to provide relief from the sweat or from thirst. His mother may have been in the crowd, given that she will be at the foot of the cross.

The way to Calvary is the icon of Christian life. It shows us Jesus, his cross, his love, his example. We follow him intent on observing him to learn how to imitate him and be his followers. The devotion of the Way of the Cross supports us in our journey. After the Eucharist and the sacraments, it is one of the most fruitful ways of commemorating the Passion of Jesus.

*O Jesus, help me to make my life a true "following" of you. May I never be led astray by other models.*

I want to consider my life, my family's and community's life, the daily happenings of my country and of all of humanity an expression of the Way of the Cross. I would like to recognize in them the different stations, till the fifteenth—the resurrection.

## SCENE 3: MISGUIDED TEARS

We can err even in the way we follow Jesus.

In the crowd that follows him beating their breasts there are women who weep for him. They are not hired mourners, nor are they members of a hypothetical confraternity of a good death. Jesus would not have paid attention to them. They are Jewish women from Jerusalem, whom Lk distinguishes from those who have come from Galilee. They are not against Jesus. They demonstrate affection and compassion.

Jesus addresses them in a severe tone, unusual in Lk's style: "Daughters of Jerusalem, do not weep for me, but weep for yourselves and for your children," 23:28. He does not scorn their lament; it is positive, since it expresses dissociation from the rejection uttered by the leaders and by part of the crowd. Jesus takes advantage of the moment to pronounce a prophecy on the fate of Jerusalem and of those who will be destroyed with it for having rejected the Messiah, and who are sons of these women.

It has nothing to do with consolation, as we say when we announce the eighth station of the cross. It shocks us and makes us realize that remaining closed to God's love has tremendous consequences. Perhaps Lk uses this poignant language because while he is writing his Gospel the destruction of Jerusalem and the Roman massacres of the Jewish people are still fresh in his mind. The early Church interpreted these events as God's punishment for the rejection of the Messiah.

"The days are coming when they will say: 'Blessed are those who are barren, and the wombs that never gave birth, and the breasts that never nursed!'" 23:29. Women who do not have children will have no one to cry over when young men are slaughtered at war.

Jesus concludes his prophetic judgment with a proverb whose precise meaning escapes us: "For if they do this when the wood is green, what will happen when it is dry?" 23:31. It most probably means: If Jesus, righteous and innocent, is condemned, what will happen to those who are guilty, that is, to all sinners?

These words pronounced by Jesus on the road to Calvary could leave a bitter taste in our mouths. Is it a sentence? Is there no salvation for these women? This would go against Lk's theology. They are beating their breasts, and upon Jesus' death they will receive the grace of true repentance. Lk cautions us of the wrong way to approach Jesus' Passion. Tears of compassion for the Crucified Jesus are useless without tears of repentance for our sins. Jesus understands and accepts Peter's tears, but he intends to purify the tears of the women of Jerusalem.

It is not enough to be moved to tears by Jesus' Passion. A change in our lives is necessary; that is, we must eliminate the causes of the Passion in ourselves and in the world. It is not enough to be compassionate towards those who suffer, but it is necessary to understand that when the suffering is unjust we must try to eliminate it.

*O my Jesus, teach me to weep for myself and for my sins. Help me to overcome them, as a fruit of my meditation upon your Passion.*

I must ask myself if I am capable of accepting my own passion: limitations, adversities, flaws, illnesses; and if I am capable of sharing in and alleviating the crosses which burden others. Thus I will be able to understand if my relationship with Jesus' Passion allows me to grow.

SCENE 4: JESUS AND HIS CROSS

Jn offers another approach to Jesus' journey to Calvary. The end of the trial, the journey and the execution are linked in a flash by actions that have as subjects only personal pronouns which refer to the leaders of the Jews.

"They" had led Jesus to Pilate, refusing to enter the praetorium. Pilate handed him over to "them" to be crucified. "They" took him to Calvary and crucified him. It is not until Jn 19:23 that we become aware of the presence of soldiers who did "their" work. But the evangelist is more interested in theological than in historical truth. "They" are responsible and guilty for Jesus' death, whoever the executioners may be.

The relationship between Jesus and his cross is unique. "He went out, bearing his own cross, to the place called the place of the skull," 19:17. There is no mention of help by the Cyrenean nor of Jesus' weakness. No one comes to his assistance. There is no need. Jesus is master of his own destiny. The cross is his, and he carries it.

The second station of the way of the cross shows us Jesus who takes the cross on his shoulders. It means that he shoulders the world, humanity, the destiny of each one of us and goes on. His life and his mission are to carry the cross.

Commentators think that Jn is alluding to Isaac who carries the wood on which he is supposed to burn in sacrifice, or that Jn wants to offer an example of a teacher who is courageous and irrepressible. Jn also deals with the theme of following Christ, although with less insistence than Lk. "If any one would serve me, let him follow me; and where I am, there shall my servant likewise be," Jn 12:26, that is, on the cross.

According to some, the exact translation is not that Jesus carries the cross "by himself," but "for himself." That is, like a tool he has chosen and which is necessary to accomplish something very important. Thus Jesus carries the cross not as one who has been condemned to death and cannot escape death, even though he does it as a hero, but because he has chosen to use it to realize his plan to save the world. Had he not said that no one takes his life, but that he has the power to give it and to take it back, cf. Jn 10:17-18?

It is an intriguing interpretation, not to be excluded.

The cross always belongs to Jesus, whether carried by the Cyrenean or by others, willingly or compelled. He is the first to take it upon himself voluntarily, to give it value and to teach us to do likewise. This manner of perceiving the cross is his creation and this cross is always his, even when we carry it. The cross is something that we do not appreciate and would avoid at any cost. But we do not succeed.

Jesus did not refuse the cross, but rather loved it. He shouldered the crosses that we do not want to carry, and he did not deserve to. All the crosses of all those who are crucified in the world belong to Jesus. When we help carry them, we help Jesus.

*O Jesus, to love life and to enjoy its values I must learn to love the cross. Teach me this lesson, the most important of my existence.*

I promise to ask if in me or around me there are crosses which do not yet belong to Jesus, because they are not accepted with love. As material well-being increases, our ability to explain the cross and to accept it decreases. Meditation on Jesus' Passion in these situations is essential. I will commit myself to transforming all the crosses I meet into the cross of Jesus.

# II. THE CROSS

Mt 27:33-56     Mk 15:22-41     Lk 23:33-49     Jn 19:17b-37

## SCENE 1: THEY CRUCIFIED HIM

**Reflect.** It is not even a major issue. At best it is for some a subordinate one. Thus the evangelists recount the horrendous torture of nailing Jesus to the cross, and of his being lifted up.

We are used to meditating upon this event with grief-stricken emotions; we imagine the nails penetrating the living flesh, the condemned gasping and writhing in agony, the lacerated tendons and nerves, the blood that squirts and then flows silently. Jesus says not a word, only prays. Thus the scene has been described and represented in every imaginable expression of art and devotion down through the centuries.

There is nothing of this in the Gospels. More attention is dedicated to the division of the garments, to the insults and to the inscription on the cross, than to the crucifixion.

Mt: "And when they had crucified him," they divided his garments, 27:35.

Mk: "And they crucified him," and divided his garments, 15:24.

Lk: "There they crucified him, and the criminals," 23:33.

Jn: They went to Calvary and "there they crucified him," 17:18.

It is over. The reader could easily have missed it. To get an idea, to imagine what took place we must rely on history. Here we find descriptions of ancient crucifixions, how they took place and how the condemned reacted.

117

Jesus is nailed to the crossbeam, the transversal part of the cross. Two soldiers nail his wrists while two others hold his body still. Then all four raise the crossbeam with the condemned man on it and hook it onto the vertical pole already planted in the ground. Then they nail the feet to the wood, with one or two nails. Jesus is there, crucified, with death being nailed into his body. His agony is full of lessons. Let us follow it with all the love of which we are capable.

During the agony our attention turns to what is happening both around the Crucified and within his heart, this second made perceptible through his words.

Why don't the evangelists dedicate any attention to Jesus' physical pain? It is immense in magnitude and precious in value because it is the means of our salvation.

They presume all this. They know that the readers are aware of the agony of the crucifixion because they have seen this spectacle frequently. Many of them were probably present at the execution of the two thousand zealots who had attempted an insurrection and whom the Romans had hung on crosses along the road from Jerusalem to Bethlehem. Everyone knows that it is the most degrading of sentences such that, like flagellation, it cannot be inflicted upon Roman citizens but only on slaves and foreigners.

The evangelists want above all to illustrate Jesus' love for the Father and for humanity, his faithfulness to his own identity and mission, his courage and consistency in choosing to give up his life for us. In addition, they accentuate the unrelenting rejection of God's love, coming from the world of sin, which is also in each of us.

The pain of the Crucified has another name—love. In Jesus, the experience of pain is inferior to the experience of love which consumes him on the cross. He is nailed by love. He is consumed by love. He will be overcome by love which brings him to offering his life such that it becomes life for the world. If it were not like this, suffering on its own would not be redemptive.

For Jesus, to be crucified means to be in love with the Father and with humanity. It is the powerful source of energy from which life comes for all, and each of us is tied to it by a thread. It is a sea, an ocean, a fire of love and pain, a love filled with pain or a painful love, as St. Paul of the Cross used to say.

Mt and Mk, however, give disconcerting glimmers of Jesus' interior affliction also, as we will see.

**Pray.** *O Jesus, help me to understand that in the human story there is always something which is greater than moral or physical suffering: it is love. You fulfilled and manifested it. Help me to gradually experience it, through your example and your help.*

**Promise.** The Crucified calls me to revisit the values upon which I have based my life. I ask him to give me the grace to make love for God and for my brothers and sisters a priority, beginning with my family members, relatives, friends and colleagues. With God's love no one is poor or lost, even if he or she is on the cross. Without God's love no one can be rich.

## Scene 2: Do not touch the tunic

According to Roman tradition, two gestures framed the crucifixion: one before and one after. The first consisted in offering to the condemned an anaesthetic drink, the second in dividing his garments among the soldiers who had him in their custody. Mt and Mk recount the first, while all four evangelists mention the second, recognizing in it the realization of various situations of the Righteous One of Israel or of the Servant of God as described in the prophets and in the psalms.

Nowadays, we have chemical anaesthetics which nullify the most atrocious of pains, even death. In Jesus' time, only natural pain relievers existed. They offer him "wine mingled with gall," Mt 27:34, or "wine mingled with myrrh," Mk 15:23. But Jesus does not drink. He wants to maintain control of his mind and of his body's sensitivity.

This drink, as all the evangelists relate, is different from the vinegar they offer Jesus during the long hours of agony which he will accept.

The garments of the condemned belong to the crucifiers—perhaps a way of compensating them for their poor wages. Psalm 22 (Hebrew enumeration; 21 in the Greek enumeration of the Septuagint and of the Latin Vulgate) mentions the stripping of his garment as one of the sufferings of the Righteous One of Israel. The psalm also lists diverse other humiliations that Mt quotes in his narration. It seems that this psalm exerted a special influence on Mt's entire narrative of the event of Calvary.

Jesus' garments end up like this. According to the Synoptics, they are divided and lots are cast for them. In Jn, the garments are shared, while lots are cast for the tunic. Perhaps the Synoptics are saying the same thing, but their approach is different. Jn however distinguishes, adding more hidden meanings: "When the soldiers had crucified Jesus they took his garments and made four parts, one for each soldier; plus his tunic. But the tunic was without seam, woven from top to bottom; so they said to one another: 'Let us not tear it, but cast lots for it to see whose it shall be,'" 19:23-24, and he also cites Psalm 22.

The garments were the exterior parts of dress. The tunic corresponded to personal underclothing. The preoccupation with not "tearing" the tunic brought to mind the high priest's dress, which according to Exodus 39:27-31 was to be seamless. Does Jn want to remind us that Jesus is the high priest who is offering this sacrifice? This is a fascinating and possible interpretation, even if the Letter to the Hebrews, which is entirely dedicated to Jesus' priesthood, makes no reference to such symbolism.

The garments may allude to humanity's unification brought about by Jesus' death, and to the unity of the Church. In fact, the Greek word for tearing is "schism," which means the division of a community or the breaking of communion.

It would not be unreasonable to think that the tunic had been woven by Jesus' mother, as Jewish women did for themselves, their husbands and for their children.

Thus, after being torn from the scourged body, the tunic now disappears. This is a further stripping and expropriation of the Crucified, now naked before the world. The only dignity remaining is the one given to him by the Creator.

*O my Jesus, you are stripped of your garments and humiliated. This is a further step in your becoming like us. The kenosis is almost at its end. It will be complete when they will strip life itself from you.*

It is possible to strip others, not only by taking away their garments or material possessions, which they have a right to, but also by not respecting their dignity. I must make sure that this never happens in my words and in my actions.

### SCENE 3: WHAT I HAVE WRITTEN I HAVE WRITTEN

Above the cross, over the head of the Crucified, there is an inscription which contains the identity of the condemned and the motivation for the execution. Pilate dictated it. All speak of it, yet Jn makes a proclamation of it and elaborates a scene similar to the one of the trial.

Mt: "This is Jesus the king of the Jews," 27:37.
Mk: "The king of the Jews," 15:26.
Lk: "This is the king of the Jews," 23:38.
Jn: "Jesus of Nazareth, the king of the Jews," 19:19.

While the Synoptics mention it as a procedural detail, without conferring too much importance upon it, Jn makes a case of it. The content of the inscription must be well assimilated. For him, the wording is a new proclamation of Jesus' kingship, more solemn than the one at the conclusion of the trial in the praetorium, because it is proclaimed in the presence of the entire world and in all the languages spoken during the international occasion of the paschal feast: Hebrew is the official and liturgical language, Greek and Latin are the languages of business. Aramaic, the language of the people and of the home, is missing, but in this case it is not necessary.

The motive of the condemnation is put in terms that ridicule the leaders of the Jews, who notice it and complain: "Do not write: 'The king of the Jews,' but, 'This man said I am the king of the Jews,'" 19:21. Pilate, fed up with the Jews and the whole ordeal, cuts them short: "What I have written I have written," 19:22.

He has taken his revenge. It is a matter of spite and of rancor which gives the scene such great effect. Truth explodes notwithstanding the intentions of the actors, both the Jews and Pilate. Just as at the moment of condemnation Jesus emerged as king, now at the moment of the crucifixion he appears again as king. Everyone can read it and everyone must understand it. Praetorium and Calvary: even the two literary structures are parallel.

Praetorium: Jesus exits the praetorium and moves towards the place called Gabbatha, that is, a platform or elevation on a stone pavement. Pilate is seated or he asks Jesus to sit and says: "Here is your king." The people shout: "Away with him, away with him! Crucify him!"

Calvary: Jesus exits the city and goes towards the place called Golgotha, that is, the place of the skull. They crucify him and Pilate writes: "The king of the Jews." They yell: "Do not write 'king' but 'he called himself king.'"

The two moments of Jesus' eradication, the death sentence and the execution, coincide with the two proclamations of his kingship, which correspond to the two rejections by the Jews. The irony of the contrasts is rending.

Two others are crucified with him, "one on either side, and Jesus between them," 19:18. Shortly he will speak his last words, and the signs of his kingship will no longer be paradoxical.

The crucifixion is the enthroning of the king. The other two crucified with him are the escorts, the followers, the assistants.

122

The inscription is the acclamation of his royal identity. The languages are the universal proclamation of his kingship. Pilate's affirmation indicates that Jesus' kingship emerges despite the rejection of the Jews and the corruption of the Romans. The seven words pronounced by Jesus on the cross are his final teaching and the last will of the king.

His royalty is striking notwithstanding his apparent defeat and the prevalence of darkness.

At the foot of the Crucified, who is still silent and immersed in prayer, lies the world agitated and restless because of him. This is truly a sign of contradiction.

*O Jesus, strengthen my faith so that I may recognize you even in the disfigurement of the cross. May I perceive and respect the identity of all human beings even when disfigured by sin and exploited by other human beings.*

Each time I focus on ephemeral values like success, money, pleasures and other material goods, I am serving idols and refusing to accept Jesus' identity. I must always be vigilant and perceptive enough to understand where and to what point this is happening in my life.

SCENE 4: INSULTS HURLED

Love and the refusal of love are the two realities that collide on Calvary. The Crucified reveals and offers the love of God. A part of humanity is obstinate in its refusal and contempt of this love.

In Jn and partly in Lk the greatness and the triumph of love stand out. Mt and Mk appear frightened by the enormity of the refusal.

In Jn the refusal is expressed only by the opposition of the Jews to the equivocal inscription posted by Pilate. Lk reports the scornful gestures of his Synoptic colleagues but attenuates them, and among them he includes Pilate's inscription.

For Mt and Mk the insults directed to the Crucified are not hurled at him haphazardly, but are logically sequenced, in three movements of diverse origin and content. They are symmetrical to the accusations which had emerged in the religious and civil trials and to the insults which covered Jesus at that time. The two evangelists appear more impressed by the virulence of the rejection than by the behavior of the Crucified.

Here is a rundown of the insults and of the revilers, according to the Synoptics.

*First series, the passers-by.*

Having heard that Jesus has proclaimed himself Lord of the temple and Son of God, they challenge him: "You who would destroy the temple and rebuild it in three days, save yourself! If you are the Son of God, come down from the cross," Mt 27:40. Their provocation offers two solutions to two desperate situations: if you are able to destroy the temple you must also be able to save yourself; if you are the Son of God, come down. In its syllogistic form the defeat is shocking: If you were God, you would come down; you do not come down, therefore you are not God.

These biting comments are accompanied by "shaking their heads," a jeer which according to Psalm 22 is directed at the Righteous One of Israel, who continues to trust in God. In Mk we can trace it through the derisive "Aha," typical of the prayer of lamentation.

Who can imagine the repercussions these attacks have on Jesus' heart? He listens from the cross: "If you are the Son of God…." The words are identical to those that Satan whispered to him in the desert: If you are the Son of God throw yourself down, turn these stones into bread. Satan is once again on the attack, in the words of these passers-by. Satan is at the foot of the cross.

From their point of view they are right. If one has so much power, he could use it for himself. But to follow this logic would indicate the most scandalous misunderstanding of the Gospel.

Nailed to the cross, Jesus is putting into practice the heart of the Gospel, already announced in words: "Whoever would save his life will lose it; and whoever loses his life for my sake and that of the Gospel will save it," Mk 8:35.

This is Jesus at his best. Demanding that he descend from the cross would mean to divest him of his power. How can anyone dare challenge him: save yourself by coming down from the cross, when he affirmed that he who saves himself in such a manner loses everything? Instead, by losing his life for love of the Gospel as he is doing, he saves himself and humanity. This is his logic and wisdom, which the apostle Paul will develop in 1 Cor 2:1-5. The attempt to separate him from the cross pursues him even now that he is nailed to it. But it will not prevail.

*O Jesus, if I look at you on the cross with human logic I will never be able to grasp the meaning of your choice. Purify and strengthen my faith so that I may understand the essence of the Gospel, which is in the cross.*

Often I would do anything to avoid certain sufferings and apparent defeats. I must evaluate all the situations of my life in the light of faith. They can be unique opportunities to mature and grow in my following of the Crucified.

## SCENE 5: INSULTS SHARPER THAN NAILS

The insults hurled at Jesus on the cross are more piercing than the nails. He is wounded by multiple crucifixions: of his body, of his human dignity, of his divine identity.

*The second series, the "chief priests with the scribes and elders."*
They salaciously infer: "He saved others; he cannot save himself. He is the king of Israel; let him come down from the cross and we will believe him. He trusts in God; let God deliver him now, if he desires him; for he said, I am the Son of God!" Mt 27:41-43; cf. Mk 15:31-32.

Should we believe that the entire Sanhedrin, seventy people draped in black like black crows, rushed beneath the cross to yell such indecencies? It is historically unlikely but the evangelists, as usual, are more concerned with theology than history. It seems incredible that opposition and rejection can reach such a point. Only the most insolent among them would be able to spew up such insults.

In the first instance, they repeat the insults of the passersby about Jesus' power to save others while not being able to save himself. What an affront!

Second, they elaborate the provocation with a more sophisticated theological argument: if he is the king of Israel—and the Christ, adds Mk—let him come down from the cross, so that we may see and believe.

In the third part of the same argument, which is reported by Mt only, the challenge shifts to trust in God. The affront is reinforced with quotations from Psalm 22 and from the Book of Wisdom 2:20, to offend Jesus in his innermost identity as Son of God.

Once again a whirlwind of insults. All the titles used by the Gospels to refer to Jesus are brought up: Christ, Messiah, king of Israel, Son of God. He claimed these titles for himself and yet he ended up on the cross. To prove that they are true, a miracle would be necessary, like descending from the cross. It would be the irrefutable demonstration of his divine power.

It is always the same logic. How could the human mind understand that dying on the cross implies a greater power than descending from it? It is the power of love.

Also the second wave of insults is an attack on the logic of the cross, more violent than the previous one. These villains have not understood anything about following Jesus. Everything butts up against it and falls to pieces—the scandal of the cross.

To the human mind only a Messiah without a cross would be acceptable, but this does not exist in God's mind, and it is impossible after the wreckage of sin. Everybody tried to get rid

127

of the cross: Peter, the disciples, the crowd, the Sanhedrin, the passers-by, the soldiers, the crucified colleagues, and Satan, the chief orchestrator. Only after Jesus dies will some of them begin to understand.

The content of *the third series of insults* against Jesus is not described by Mt and Mk. They say that the offences came from "the robbers who were crucified with him." According to Mt they more or less repeat what they hear from others, 27:44.

Lk reports two series of insults against the Crucified. One comes from the crowd, who drive home again the issue of saving himself if he is the Christ. The other comes from the soldiers who refer to him as king of the Jews, 23:35-38, the only title they can understand as Romans.

The irony further underlines that all of Jesus' titles are confirmed while an effort is made to deny them, as occurs in Jn with the title of kingship.

The insults launched against the Crucified express humanity's difficulty in understanding the logic of the cross. To this day they are still being hurled against him in history, for instance by scientific development which considers itself self-sufficient, by those in power who try to be omnipotent, by cultures that only rely upon reason and success, by Christians who think they can reconcile the cross with everything.

*O Jesus, I thank you for your fidelity to the cross, which is fidelity to love. Because you are on the cross to the end, now you can stand by my cross and by the crosses of humanity to the end of time.*

There is only one thing the Crucified cannot do: free us from our crosses. We have built them by abusing our freedom. But the Crucified does much more than this: he takes our crosses upon himself and he carries them with us. This is why he did not want to descend from the cross. I must remember this in carrying my cross, so I will feel stronger and motivated by love.

## Scene 6: A gift called forgiveness

Now our attention, along with that of all Christians down through the ages, turns to the last words of the Crucified.

Of the seven sentences pronounced by Jesus during his agony, three are reported by Lk, three by Jn and one by Mt and Mk. According to the traditional numeration of the seven phrases, the one on forgiveness comes first and is reported by Lk.

"They crucified him and the criminals. And Jesus said, 'Father, forgive them, for they know not what they do,'" Lk 23:33-34. It appears from the context that Jesus is pronouncing these words while being nailed to the cross, thus he intends the executioners. But it is obvious that also those insulting him at that moment are recipients of his forgiveness, and so is humanity of all times, you and me included.

In many ancient manuscripts these words have been suppressed, but they are present in others and in all the commentaries of the Fathers of the Church, therefore they are to be considered authentic. They fit in with Lk's style and theology. Maybe some copyists, still angry with the Jews for rejecting Jesus, omitted these words as being too generous. Or, if we admit that Lk writes after the destruction of the temple—and this was considered a punishment for the rejection of the Messiah—some copyists may have found it difficult to reconcile that event with these words of forgiveness.

The purpose of the sentence is not only to excuse or attenuate the responsibility of the Jews, but above all to confirm the Christian need of forgiveness. Jesus had formulated it in his Sermon on the Plain: "Love your enemies, do good to those who hate you, bless those who curse you, pray for those who abuse you," Lk 6:27-28.

The Master knows that for the disciple this is the most difficult lesson to learn. Therefore he gives an example, to show that it is possible even in the most impossible of situations: forgive those who are killing you. In Acts 7:60, Lk will demonstrate, reporting the case of Stephen, that a true disciple is able to follow the Master to that point.

From the heart of the dying Jesus we are offered forgiveness and are requested to forgive. While dying on the cross Jesus reveals God's love to us. It goes beyond all possibilities of love imaginable by the human mind. He loves even when not loved or rejected or killed. His love is a gift whose ultimate expression is forgiveness. It is a super gift. It is a gift that on his part never fails. Only our persistence in rejecting it may render his love unsuccessful. This would be our condemnation, including hell.

We need to feel the transforming power of this word. It cannot be limited to the four ignorant executioners, but it is for us and for always, even today. We do not know what we are doing when we refuse to love what life offers us, or when we wear ourselves out over values which do not last, or when we forget to search in God for the only relationship which fulfills our lives. Our misery is so profound that God cannot but forgive it.

The weakening of the sense of sin makes us lose the sense of forgiveness. Also for this Jesus forgives us. If we miss the experience of being forgiven, our capacity of forgiving is also diluted. The two aspects are inseparable: we must forgive because we are forgiven; we are forgiven to the extent that we forgive. Jesus taught us this also in the prayer of the Our Father.

*O Jesus, forgive me for neglecting forgiveness. Help me to rediscover its greatness and to experience its joy.*

I must examine if in my life there are wounds that are still open because of my inability to forgive. Before running to the psychologist it would be better to spend some time at the foot of the Crucifix. It is not expensive and it can be more effective.

## Scene 7: The thief who stole heaven

The condemnation of criminals is a source of consolation in society even today. We feel it whenever we hear that a corrupt public official, mafia boss, assailant, kidnapper or rapist is caught and punished. There are full-time and incidental criminals. Society tends to remove them as a threat of infection.

In Jesus' time a capital execution was one of the few occasions of public spectacle in which people could vent their anger and frustration. This is also why around the three crucified men on Calvary people gathered attracted by different interests.

In their turn the condemned often retaliated with insults and maledictions. This is happening also in this case, except for the one crucified in the middle. Lk reports it with exceptional skill, both literary and theological, making of it a drama within a drama.

One of the two, according to tradition the one on the left, insults Jesus echoing what he hears from others: "Are you not the Christ? Save yourself and us!" Lk 23:39. The other also, according to Mk, at the beginning hurled insults at Jesus, but at a certain moment he distances himself from the general mood of hatred and insolence that infests the scene. Perhaps he has been struck by Jesus' previous words and by his prayerful silence. In his deepest intuition he probably perceives that the man in the center must be motivated by love. He starts by rebuking his companion: "Do you not fear God, since you are under the same sentence of condemnation? And we indeed justly. But this man has done nothing wrong," 23:40-41.

The absence of the fear of God makes us arrogant, thus closed to forgiveness. Fear of God makes us feel the tenderness of his mercy, as Mary sings in the Magnificat, Lk 1:50. The crucified thief has now become the "good thief." He recognizes that he is guilty and affirms that Jesus is innocent, assuming it from Jesus' attitude since they left the praetorium with the cross on their shoulders. He concludes that a man who behaves in such a manner must be of great stature.

There is another way of proving that one is king, besides descending from the cross. It is to stay on it as he does. Now the thief surrenders to the risk of faith. "Jesus, remember me when you come into your kingdom," 23:42. This leap in the dark does not end up in the abyss, but in the arms of love. The answer is immediate and supremely generous, in the language of important revelations: "Amen, I say to you, today you will be with me in paradise," 23:43.

He has been saved. If one claims salvation as a right and a challenge he won't be saved. If one asks for it recognizing his own sins and surrendering to love, he is saved. The "good thief" has become a disciple and is among the first to follow Jesus.

In reporting this second word, Lk again proclaims Jesus' innocence and demonstrates the saving power of his death. After these two words, it is difficult to understand why some scholars still maintain that in Lk the power of redemption does not derive from the death but only from the resurrection of Jesus. On the contrary, it is clear that salvation springs from his wounds and his love, like the flow of blood which is "poured out for you," 22:20.

Jesus, who has always been a friend of sinners and generous in forgiving them, chooses to be in their company even when dying. And he takes one of them with him as he leaves this world. He is the infinite largess of God personified. A single heartbeat of love before dying is sufficient to take hold of paradise and enter it by full right. So great is God's longing that all be saved.

*O Jesus, the generosity of your forgiveness invites us to a limitless hope. You were asked to remember a condemned thief and you offered him a place with you in paradise.*

The different fates of the two thieves give us further insight to understanding the meaning of the cross. In the human condition the cross is inevitable. But carrying it with Jesus saves us, while bearing it without Jesus may lead to despair. With Jesus it leads us on high, while without him it makes us fall into the depths. How am I carrying my cross? How do I share the cross of others?

SCENE 8: HIS MOTHER WAS THERE

Calvary appears deserted. Jn focuses on Jesus' mother and the disciple whom he loved to convey an important message—the third word.

The Synoptics also speak of women beneath the cross, but they mention them only after the death of Jesus, not before. The list is more or less the same. They all name Mary Magdalene, but only Jn concentrates on the presence of his mother: "Standing by the cross of Jesus were his mother and his mother's sister, Mary the wife of Clopas and Mary Magdalene," Jn 19:25.

His mother Mary was always close to Jesus even though she is mentioned only rarely—when he is born and when he dies and a few other times. What is obvious does not need repeating.

"When Jesus saw his mother, and the disciple whom he loved standing near, he said to his mother, 'Woman, behold your son,'" 19:26.

Especially in this last century, an enormous effort has been made to interpret these words in order to grasp with certainty their full content.

This is obviously not a simple family matter—a dying son providing for his mother's care. Jn has never worried about these things. In addition, the issue is expressed with the language generally reserved for solemn revelations, usually introduced with "Behold" or "Amen": "Behold a day will come", "Behold, you will conceive and bear a son", "Behold the Lamb of God."

"Woman" may sound cold to us at this moment. Jesus used this title only with women he did not know, and once with his mother at Cana. In fact, Jn links these two incidents. At Cana, with the strength of her faith, she drew Jesus out of his anonymity and forced him to anticipate the hour of his own manifestation with the miracle of the water changed into wine. In a certain sense, in that occasion she "generated" the faith of the disciples, who as a result also came to believe. On Calvary, with the hour of his manifestation at its climax, she is about to discover the ultimate horizons of her own mission.

Three times in two verses Jn recalls that she is Jesus' mother, and "your mother" in general. Therefore "woman" indicates her maternal role.

Many Fathers of the Church taught that Jesus alluded to the Woman-Eve, who signifies the life bearer. In this case the meaning of Jesus' words would be: Just as Eve is at the source of all human life and is the mother of all human beings, so you Woman-Mary are at the source of the new humanity which is being born from my death on the cross. She is the Woman-Humanity at the origin of life and without which there is no life.

Some contemporary scholars, referring to medieval interpreters including St. Thomas Aquinas, think that the title indicates the Woman-Mother of the eschatological Israel, that is Israel fully and definitively saved. A Christian author of the end of the first century refers to this "new Israel" as the community of Jesus, the Church. The woman of Calvary is therefore Israel that becomes the Church of Jesus Christ, the hinge between the old and the new, the best of the old and of the new, the first believer and the first disciple, first born of the Church and at the same time Mother of the Church. What is not physically possible, that a woman be mother of herself, is symbolically possible according to this word of Jesus reported by Jn.

Jesus completes this third word by addressing his disciple, adding: "Behold your mother," 19:27.

The "disciple whom Jesus loved" is an expression used six times only by Jn, only in the narrative of the Passion, and always coupled with Peter except in this case. Whoever he may be, he must be the ideal disciple, mature, in full communion with Jesus, to the point of sharing his mother. He is the model disciple, the icon for the community of disciples.

There is no doubt that, with this word of Jesus, Jn intends to convey to the Church the experience of the spiritual maternity of Mary, which his community was already living.

*O my Jesus, with this word you transformed all that is Christian into being "Marian" also. Our love for you and our following of you must necessarily bear the imprint of your mother.*

I must verify if the relationship with Mary in my life is according to Jesus' intentions. That is, she must always be present as my mother.

## SCENE 9: THE ULTIMATE ANNUNCIATION

The first annunciation occurred when the archangel Gabriel told Mary that she was to become the mother of God. The second, John Paul II observes, took place when the prophet Simeon foretold that a sword would pierce her soul because of this child. These are two phases of Mary's walk of faith, in which God intervened to help her discover and accept new dimensions of her mission.

Thus we are allowed to use the category of annunciation to reflect upon the turning points in the journey of Mary's faith as reported in the Gospels. Each new immersion into the mystery of her Son is an annunciation.

Another annunciation came about when Jesus, lost and found in the temple, made clear to her that his first preoccupation was to be about his heavenly Father' business. She took what he said very seriously and "kept all these things in her heart," Lk 2:51, in silence, for the decades of Jesus' hidden life in Nazareth.

Yet another annunciation took place at Cana, when she sensed that she would have a role in her Son's mission. She did not understand fully how, but her faith left no doubt that somehow this would be so. This would be confirmed on Calvary.

Still another annunciation was probably when she anxiously

tried to stay near her Son during his public ministry, but he sent a message to her saying that the best way of being his mother and of remaining close to him was to do the will of the Father.

On Calvary she embraces in faith the last annunciation that completes all the others. It comes neither from an angel nor from a holy prophet, but from her own Son. What is it? "Woman, behold your son." She will be not only mother to Jesus but to his disciples as well. She is to be the mother not only of the Head but also of the members of the Body, potentially of the whole human race.

Jesus is dying, and in the agony of love he generates salvation. Mary also is losing all that she has in life, her Son, and in the shared agony of love she becomes the mother of those who are saved. Jesus has chosen to associate her to his suffering while he is fulfilling the will of the Father and saving the world.

Now Mary understands all that was implied when she agreed at the first annunciation to become the mother of God. Now she is at the peak of her maturity as a woman, a mother and a believer. Since she always "stood" by Jesus, she assimilated his mystery and gradually came to understand the implications of her own vocation and mission.

She always answered with the same willingness and abandonment of her initial fiat. In the annunciation on Calvary she has the same attitude. It is at the moment of her greatest sorrow that she receives the ultimate revelation about her identity and mission. Sorrow and affliction can always be occasions for understanding God and ourselves. Trials always reveal who we are, what we are worth, and to what we are called.

As she "stood" by the cross of Jesus, Mary now "stands" by the cross of every human being. There is no cross of mine or of yours from which Mary is absent. She always helps us carry our crosses with love. This is the spiritual maternity that by faith she extends to all of us from Calvary. Whereas she generated Jesus physically and in faith, so in faith she generates us all.

"From that hour the disciple took her into his care," 19:27. Every disciple is asked to welcome Mary and establish a deep relationship with her. It is the mother-child relationship that should characterize our spiritual identity. She accepts us as her children and we take her as our mother.

At the same time Mary is to be considered one of the most precious gifts that Jesus left us, along with the life of faith, his word, the sacraments, the Eucharist, fraternal charity, et cetera.

According to Jn, this is Jesus' last important accomplishment before his death. It is part of his love to the end, as announced at the beginning of the Supper, before the washing of the feet, 13:1. In fact, soon after entrusting his work to his mother, Jesus "knowing that all was now finished," 19:28, prepares to die. The gift of his mother is part of the gift of himself.

*O Jesus, help me to look at you and to love you through the eyes and heart of your mother, since you love me and care for me with your mother's heart.*

*O mother of Jesus, you are also my mother. You are the first fruit of Jesus' Passion and now you complete it in your own suffering, an example and model for us all.*

I must learn from Mary that following the Crucified and "standing" by him entails continually discovering new dimensions of my own vocation and mission.


## SCENE 10: MY GOD, MY GOD

The tragedy heads towards a conclusion. Mk subdivides it into three phases, like the prayer in Gethsemane and Peter's denials. According to him, Jesus hangs on the cross for six hours instead of the three we can infer from the other evangelists. "It was the third hour when they crucified him," Mk 15:25. The third hour corresponds to 9:00 a.m. From nine to twelve o'clock waves of insults were hurled at the Crucified. From twelve to three p.m. darkness envelops the land. This is an apocalyptic detail used by authors to describe the death of great figures or God's interventions in history.

Today we no longer fear darkness. By the mere flip of a switch we inundate even the darkest of nights with bright light. But at that time darkness could be frightening.

According to Mt and Mk at 3:00 p.m., while the threatening gloom makes even the courageous shudder, Jesus utters the only word they report: "Then he cried out with a loud voice, 'Eloi, Eloi, lama sabachthani?,' which means, 'My God, my God, why have you forsaken me?'" Mk 15:34. Mt 27:46 has the Hebrew Eli instead of Mk's Aramaic Eloi.

This is the most disconcerting of the seven words. This moment of the Passion has terrified mystics and puzzled commentators, even more than the prayer in the garden of Gethsemane.

As far as the narratives of Mt and Mk are concerned, there is no reason for worry. They present the demise of Jesus as the death of the Righteous One of Israel, who trusts in God until the end. They have no other messages to convey unlike Lk and Jn. Their only intent is to describe the death of a human being who does not fall into despair but finds in God a vital support as his life is ebbing away.

These words of Jesus are to be found at the beginning of Psalm 22, which we should read carefully if we are to understand Mt's and Mk's Passion narratives. An ancient Christian tradition closely links the Passion of Jesus with this psalm which is long and rich in content. It expresses not only the sufferings but also the hopes of the Righteous One of Israel while being assailed by insults and threats like Jesus on the cross.

In the long hours of his agony, pierced by nails and insults, uttering words of forgiveness and making provision for those most dear to him as in a last will and testament, while death takes possession of his body with the passing of the hours, Jesus was certainly praying Psalm 22. No surprise if he cried out some verse of it.

Jewish prayer can be expressed in three ways—words, tears, loud cries. Since this psalm was a popular prayer, people knew it and used it in all the difficult moments of their history and personal life. Today we are reluctant to show that we are weak and in need of help. Even when our dear ones are facing death we feel bound to hide our true feelings, we give them the illusion that nothing is wrong, we help them with sedatives. Cultural trends regarding personal dignity or "political correctness" in our day and age restrain us from manifesting our true humanity.

The content of the psalm is twofold: lamentation in the first part, praise and thanksgiving for God's intervention in the second. If Jesus cries out one of its verses we can conclude that he is experiencing its entire content.

The prayer of lamentation was typical of the Old Testament. It called for God's intervention even with paradoxical expressions. As if to say, "My God, my God, is it possible that you have forsaken me?" the petitioner cries out the concept in order to affirm that it cannot be true. Those who knew the psalm understood that Jesus' cry was an expression of trust, to counteract the insults, one of which challenged his confidence in God.

*O Jesus, after your Passion and death, the passions and deaths of all human beings down through the ages no longer have the meaning they once had. By assuming and sharing in them yourself, you have transformed them all.*

Death is the radical poverty of human beings. Jesus experienced it in all its crudeness to help us overcome its trauma. I want to consider my life, my problems and my projects from the point of view of death. Thus I will learn to be more peaceful and detached from worldly cares.

## SCENE 11: THE CRY OF A WOUNDED HUMANITY

Is it possible to comprehend to what extent God became human? The fourth word of the Crucified reveals to us the most comprehensive understanding of this mystery. Did Jesus feel abandoned by God to the point of sharing our human experience of separation from God? Many mystics say yes even though the how remains concealed.

There is a separation from God that is caused by sin. The sinner does not realize the consequences of this alienation. If he understood them, he would already be in hell, which consists in the full awareness of having lost God forever.

It may be that Jesus, in order to atone for human sin, experienced in his human conscience the effect of estrangement from God that sinners cannot perceive. Such an experience cannot be endured by a human being in this earthly state, but could have been possible for a human being who was without sin and had assumed the consequences of sin, as had Jesus. He is truly man, though without sin, created for the happiness of communion with God.

His "cry" could thus be the desolate reaction of a creature made for God but torn away from God by sin. It may be the cry of humanity wounded by sin and impotent before it.

In Gethsemane Jesus caught a first glance of the abyss of this situation and was filled with dismay. On Calvary he reaches the supreme awareness of the true depth of this abyss, that is of the destructive power of sin, and he feels devastated by it. This is why he cries to God, without even calling him Father: How is it possible that humanity has been "forsaken" to the point of precipitating so deeply? It is like viewing a disaster area from above and feeling the anguish reverberating within oneself. Therefore, the cry is both of Jesus and of humanity, which through him is heard by the Father.

There is also a separation from God caused by God, as a purification of love. It is the one of the mystics. They are fully

141

aware of this distancing and describe it in terms that could correspond to the state of damnation. Several mystics affirm that on the cross Jesus experienced this form of the silence of God. The Father could have permitted it so that his Son could earn the highest merit in his humanity for the salvation of the world.

Thus Jesus would have experienced complete abandonment. Forsaken by humanity whom he loved to the point of assuming it: he realizes that nobody has understood him. He feels also forsaken by God, who is his own life and identity.

For this reason Jesus' cry is the synthesis of all of humanity's prayers. The *Catechism of the Catholic Church* underlines it in the section on prayer. "All the troubles, for all time, of humanity enslaved by sin and death, all the petitions and intercessions of salvation history are summed up in this cry of the incarnate word," 2606. And further ahead: "Jesus also prays for us—in our place and on our behalf. All our petitions were gathered up, once for all, in his cry on the cross and, in his resurrection, heard by the Father," 2741.

Mt and Mk speak of another wordless cry of Jesus, which coincides with his death. This cry of the God made man in his death sheds its light on our experiences of suffering and death. We also, sooner or later, find ourselves in situations in which we are about to cry: Where is God? Why this or that? Why to me? It may be a matter of abandonment, failure, irreparable break-ups, mortal wounds, the death of friends or dear ones and our own death.

Where is God? Alas! He is there, in those very things. Like on the cross.

*O my Jesus, now I understand that all of the cries that resound on earth—of the poor, the exploited, the sick, the murdered—can become prayer, and probably are, without knowing it.*

If I were aware of the degree of separation from God caused by my sins I would already be in the desperation of hell. I must be vigilant and pray that sin never take hold of my life.

## SCENE 12: THIRST

After the pain of the nails, thirst was the most excruciating torture for a crucified individual. The evangelists report that Jesus was given something to drink when he was on the cross, but Jn alone says that Jesus complained of thirst.

They gave him a drink which tasted like vinegar, probably drawing it from the canteens of the soldiers, who in the summer used an acidulous potion to quench their thirst. The people of the village where I came from used to drink it, too, before the world became invaded by Coke and other soft drinks. Jesus accepts a sip of it from the dripping sponge.

In Mt and Mk the soldiers offer him a drink following his cry of lament and abandonment. They confused Eli or Eloi, that is the name of God, with the name of the prophet Elijah, and they thought that he had invoked the saint of the impossible.

There was a common expectation that Elijah would reappear at the coming of the Messiah, but Jesus had explained that the prophet had already come in the person of John the Baptist. His role was not to free the Messiah from death, but to prepare the hearts of the people to welcome him.

In Lk the cry of abandonment is missing, and so is the misunderstanding about Elijah. The soldiers lift the sponge to Jesus' lips mocking him and saying: "If you are the king of the Jews, save yourself," 23:37.

In Jn, Jesus' mention of his thirst is set in a solemn context, after the word to his mother and to the disciple whom he loved, that leads us to think of a possible hidden meaning. "After this Jesus, knowing that all was now finished, said to fulfill the Scripture: 'I thirst,'" 19:28. It seems that he says this word to bring the Scriptures to fulfillment. In fact, in Psalms 22 and 69 there are allusions to this suffering of the Righteous One of Israel: "My tongue cleaves to my jaws," Ps 22:15; and "For my thirst they gave me vinegar to drink," Ps 69:21.

Some scholars maintain however that translating more faithfully from the original text, it should read: "After this, knowing that all the Scriptures had been fulfilled, Jesus said: 'I thirst.'" Thus his thirst does not refer to the fulfillment of the Scriptures, but to something else.

Early commentators insisted on the physical aspect of thirst, as they had to fight against heresies that denied the real human body of Jesus. But already before the end of the first millennium there are numerous interpretations concerning the spiritual aspects of Jesus' thirst. Jesus ardently longs to be united with the Father and to save humanity.

A fascinating recent interpretation sees in Jesus' thirst his longing to pour forth the Holy Spirit into the world for the continuation of his work, as he will shortly do while dying, "giving up his spirit."

All these meanings can be included because they are part of Jesus' language in the Gospel of Jn. Jesus is thirsty because his throat is dry. He also thirsts to bring to completion his work, to do the will of the Father until the end by drinking from the chalice of death. In fact, he had rebuked Peter who tried to defend him with a sword, saying, "Shall I not drink the cup which the Father has given me?" 18:11.

According to the Synoptics, in the garden of Gethsemane Jesus prayed: "Father, if it be possible, let this cup pass from me," Mt 26:39. According to Jn, on the cross Jesus burns with desire to drink that cup, to manifest his love to the end.

This appears even clearer from another symbolic allusion that Jn assembles in the gestures of quenching Jesus' thirst. Instead of putting the sponge on a reed, the soldiers place it on a branch of hyssop, which is a tender shrub. It must be difficult to keep a sponge on a cluster of leaves. But the leaves of hyssop were used by the Hebrews in Egypt to mark the doors of their houses with the blood of the paschal lamb, and so to save their families from the slaughtering of their first born. Jesus thirsts to be the new paschal lamb.

The *Catechism of the Catholic Church* interprets Jesus' thirst on the cross as God's desire for our salvation. "Jesus thirsts; his asking arises from the depths of God's desire for us," 2560.

On the cross Jesus thirsts for me, that I may find happiness with him.

*O Jesus, your thirst is your longing to show us your love to the end. It is another way to say love. May your love reach us and save us all so that no one be lost.*

As long as every human being does not live according to God's plan, Jesus will keep on crying, "I am thirsty." I must examine myself to see if my life is consistent with the commitments I have made and if it corresponds to the plan Jesus has for me. I must verify if in my work I contribute to the fulfillment of God's will in society and in history.

## SCENE 13: HE DIES A KING

At every step of his Passion narrative, from Gethsemane to the last breath on Calvary, Jn reminds us that Jesus is king. He carried the cross by himself, just like one who does not yield a precious tool he must use. He hangs on it, between two others, as if he were on the highest level of an award platform. He entrusted his community to the maternal love of his own mother. He proclaimed that by now his only longing is to overcome the limitations of the human world so that the Holy Spirit may overflow on it, and God and humanity may be reunited in one family. He completed all that he had set out to do and for which he had been sent by the Father as foretold in the Scriptures.

Now he is ready to die. He does not need to hasten because death is at his door, but death can come because he is ready for it. He is king even over death.

Having expressed his longing for fulfillment by saying, "I am thirsty," and having sipped the thirst-quenching drink, he says: "It is finished," Jn 19:30. This word makes us realize that he is at the end. Life is over, it is time to die. But the prevailing significance is that he has completed the work which he had come to do, the end and purpose of his mission. The end has been reached, the work has been finished.

A previous translation, which was probably more appropriate, said: "Everything is accomplished"—a job, homework, a book, a game, climbing a mountain, an exam, the birth of a child, a love shared. It is the moment in which one breathes happiness and contemplates the work accomplished. It is one of the most moving moments of human self-fulfillment. Everything else in life is affected by it.

Jesus is there in all his usual majesty.

"He bowed his head and gave up his spirit," Jn 19:30, "delivered over his spirit," according to the NAB, 1976. "Give up" is the same word used to indicate Jesus' handing himself over to the power of darkness, to be arrested, to the trial, to the cross and to death. "Spirit" is the same word Jesus uses to indicate the Holy Spirit.

The word certainly means that Jesus dies, but it happens because he gives himself up to death and decides to die, not because others take his life away. It is true that they arrested, tried and condemned him, but he always came out greater than his enemies. Now it appears that he is even greater than death, to which he hands himself over when he chooses.

Modern commentators have no doubt that "spirit" means not only Jesus' human soul, but also the Holy Spirit. By allowing his human spirit to leave his body, that is by giving himself up to death as a man, he delivers the Holy Spirit over to humanity. His death has now cleared the world of sin, and the Holy Spirit can resume possession of all creation.

Jn does not recount the descent of the Holy Spirit at Pentecost, as Lk does in the Acts. There, we are told that the Spirit descends from heaven as a consequence of Jesus ascending to the Father. Moreover he descends especially to confirm the mission of the Church.

In Jn the Holy Spirit is given by Jesus especially for the comprehension of his message. It is symbolized also by the water that shortly will flow from his open heart. Jesus will breathe the Spirit on the apostles on the evening of his resurrection; the moment of his death when he breathes forth his spirit is an anticipation of that event.

So Jesus breathes his last, handing his work over to the Spirit. The work of the Father for humanity is not left unguarded even for an instant. The whole Trinity cares for our salvation. The time of the historical Jesus ends. The time of the Spirit begins. Thus, at the moment of his death Jesus accomplishes the most vital act of life possible. This death is the triumph over death.

The new community is already present with Mary and the disciple. The Spirit already animates and guides it.

*O Jesus, your death is your most vital moment because in it you loved the most, giving up your life for us and thus sending your Spirit upon us. Help me to look to my death as the ultimate opportunity to express my love for you.*

To reach death saying "everything is accomplished" as Jesus did, it is necessary to be able to say it every day and in all of life's actions. I must examine if in my life everything is well accomplished. When it is not I must make reparation with contrition and penance.

## SCENE 14: HE DIES TEACHING

The time for the last lesson has come. The topic is how to die. Lk always presented Jesus as a teacher coming from God to instruct humanity on how to be human. Around him the crowds and his chosen ones have always been attentive as disciples who have much to learn. The scenario of Golgotha reflects this teacher-disciple relationship.

The evangelist omits details that do not fit in with this setting, like the cry of Jesus and the misunderstanding about Elijah. Along with the others, he does, however, mention the darkness that thickens at noon: "It was about the sixth hour, and there was darkness over the whole land," 23:44. He does so to emphasize that darkness is always linked to the end of the world or of a phase of its history. It is not a local but a cosmic occurrence.

The teacher is high on the cross as on a podium. He is spending the time of his agony in prayer, whose principal con-

149

tents have been the forgiveness for his executioners and the promise of paradise to the good thief. Now death is imminent because asphyxia is stopping his heart, probably struck by a new ischemic attack, and he is running a fever above 104°F. And what is the master doing? He is still praying—to the very end.

The tradition about the "cry" must also have been present in Lk's sources, for he also relates that the last word of Jesus was pronounced loudly as in Mt and Mk. But it has a different content: "Jesus, crying out with a loud voice, said: 'Father, into your hands I commend my spirit,'" 23:46.

The prayer is a quotation from Psalm 31:5 where the meaning swings from anguish to thanksgiving. On Jesus' lips however, it expresses the peaceful abandonment of someone who is certain that he will not fall into the abyss but into the arms of love. In fact, he puts before the quotation of the psalm the word, "Father," which in Lk always opens Jesus' prayer. Such was the case in the prayer of the garden of Gethsemane and in this very agony when he prayed for his executioners. It is clear that Lk intends to present a peaceful death, in a dignified and trusting abandonment to the Father, the kind of death that every disciple should desire and prepare for.

The relationship between Jesus and the Father always fascinated the disciples. Many times they tried to pursue the master when he disappeared from their sight to go pray, or when he appeared estranged from their company because immersed in the mystery of the Father. Therefore one time, partly curious and partly frustrated, they had asked him to teach them how to pray. They already knew how to pray because they were good Jews, but they had perceived that Jesus' prayer was something different, a thing of love, a filial relationship. And Jesus had formulated for them the prayer of the Our Father.

With his prayer on the cross, Jesus encourages each one of us to restore our relationship with the Father. Salvation is first of all the work of the Father. Jesus is a gift from the Father. It is not Jesus' intent that we center on him only, but he wants to lead us to the Father, in their love that is the Holy Spirit. We cannot forget the Father. The life of faith is a filial experience. No one else reveals Jesus' spirituality as Lk does. Always in communion with his Father, Jesus manifested his love whose ultimate expression is mercy. Now he hangs on the cross while death is imminent. He takes death in his hands, so to say, he accepts it, embraces it and makes of it the final choice of his life. What he says in words is what his heart longs for most—to return to the Father. "Having said this he breathed his last," 23:46. We have here an example of a serene and heroic death. It will be a support to many martyrs and must be thus for all of his disciples.

*O Jesus, what will become of me when I will be dead like you? May my desire to be with you and with the Father make my detachment from this life easier. Help me to look at my death with your same serenity.*

One of the causes of modern neurosis is the awareness that death cannot be avoided. The Crucified frees us from this preoccupation. He calls his death an act of love or the gift of his own life. If from now I make of death a free choice and an act of love it will not frighten me. Reflecting on death may become a fruitful way of reflecting on life.

## SCENE 15: HE DIES LIKE A MAN

He dies as the majority of human beings die, with the frightened and powerless look of one who asks why. He dies without wanting to die, since we are never ready for this passage. He does not rebel or despair, but he cries out God's name as his only security while sinking into the unknown abyss of the mystery.

Also rich in teaching and comfort, this, more or less, is Jesus' death as presented by Mt and Mk.

Mk, consistent with his austere style abruptly ends: "Jesus

uttered a loud cry and breathed his last," 15:37. After the cry of abandonment and the sip of the vinegary drink, death falls suddenly in a sharp wordless lament. Trust in God does not fail, but the fierce assault of death is fully felt.

Many efforts have been made to interpret and give sense to that final "loud cry." Was it the cry of the dying Righteous One? Or was it a cry of victory or liberation or exorcism?

Perhaps it is better to leave to the words their sense of stark dismay. Jesus already explained during the Supper the meaning of his death. His life would be given up for all, the gift of his body and of his blood. Now that death arrives, he experiences the pain and desolation of it known to all the poor abandoned people of the world who are not assisted or mourned by anyone.

No other passage of the New Testament expresses Jesus' humanity with such realism. But it also reveals illuminating aspects of the death of the God made man. He does not choose a heroic death, but a deplorable and miserable one, accepted with the cry that appeals to God for an explanation of this unjust and cruel occurrence.

The cry with which he accepts this inglorious reality will be the reason for his glory. Even dying like this may be a revelation of God. Someone will realize it and will point it out shortly.

Jesus' death in Mt is similar to the death recounted by Mk, but with attenuated tones. "Jesus cried again with a loud voice and yielded up his spirit," 27:50. Here also the cry is different from the previous lamentation: "My God, my God, why have you forsaken me?" 27:46.

Perhaps Jesus is praying all of Psalm 22, with "supplications, loud cries and tears," Heb 5:7. Maybe this final cry is another quotation from the same psalm, for instance, verse 24: "He has not hid his face from me but has heard me when I cried to him." Thus Jesus dies with the attitude of the Righteous One who surrenders to God, feeling protected by him.

Also the description of death lends itself to a gentler interpretation. "He yielded up his spirit," instead of the austere "he breathed his last," may hint at the biblical vision of human life. The spirit is the life given by God at the beginning of creation. It is handed over to us for the extent of our lives, but it belongs to him. When life ends we must give it back to God. When God takes it back, life ends. By giving back his spirit, Jesus accomplishes his final act of obedience to his Father.

Jesus experiences human death in all its brutality: with dismay but in dignified acceptance according to Mk; with acceptance and abandonment according to Mt. He is close to all who die without frills: those who die because of wars and violence; those who die without religion, who do not understand why one is born, lives and dies; those who die suddenly, just in time to realize that they are not ready. For all, his death has become a source of grace.

*O Jesus, the extreme poverty of your death helps me to understand that from that moment onwards no death is necessarily meaningless. If in dying we are able to surrender to someone it means that life does not end.*

Today's culture has overcome many taboos, but not the one of death. People do not want to speak of it, or they allude to it with gestures of exorcism. The Passion of Jesus teaches also how to have a positive relationship with death.

## SCENE 16: BUT HE IS GOD

Jesus had just breathed his last when suddenly Calvary was shaken by a cosmic confirmation that Jesus was right. The enemies have hardly begun celebrating their victory when the earth imposes signs of Jesus' own victory.

According to the Synoptics these signs are apparent in nature, in the temple and in people's change of mind. According to Jn the signs emanate from the body of the Crucified.

Only Mt speaks of the cosmic signs that erupt at Jesus' death. "The earth shook and the rocks were split. The tombs also were opened," 27:51-52. These earthly reactions are typical of the manifestations of God. By mentioning the opening of the tombs Mt intends to urge his community, discouraged because of its rejection by Judaism, to trust in the power of God who is able to give victory even after death.

"Many bodies of the saints who had fallen asleep were raised, and coming out of the tombs, after his resurrection, they appeared to many," 27:52-53. The author realizes that his enthusiasm has led him to anticipate events that could not have taken place before Christ's resurrection, therefore he clarifies by inserting the clause "after his resurrection." He wants to demonstrate that the Father's response is immediate, not postponed to the resurrection.

Jesus' death out of love has redemptive value in itself and is the reason for his victory, even though chronologically this victory will be manifested later on, in the resurrection.

The Synoptics mention the tearing of the veil of the temple. It was not the curtain that separated the exterior courtyard from the sanctuary, but the one that enclosed the Holy of Holies, to which only the high priest had access once a year.

What is the meaning of this disquieting sign? Does this mean that God, enraged by humanity's rejection of his Son, tears his garments as the high priest had torn his own robe at Jesus' declaration of his divine identity?

In Lk the splitting of the veil precedes Jesus' death, while in Mt and Mk it follows. Therefore in Lk it could allude to a rift in the heavens or to the crumbling of the wall of enmity between God and humanity. Looking through that rift Jesus could have seen the face of the Father and cried out his sense of abandonment, as the martyr Stephen will do, following his master's example, Ac 7:55.

In all of the Synoptics this event contains a judgment on the fate of the temple of Jerusalem. Its end had been announced. With Jesus' death it was brought about. Even if the evangelists, or some of them, know of the material destruction of the temple, which occurred in 70 A.D., what they intend to point out is the end of the temple's religious function. There is no longer a need for it. God no longer dwells in the Holy of Holies, but in the most holy body of his crucified Son, and also in his extended body formed by all who belong to him through faith and the sacraments.

The tearing of the veil from top to bottom signifies that God has changed his dwelling place, he has moved to new quarters, not made by human hands but constructed on faith and love. Henceforth he will abide in the new community that flows from the heart of the Crucified, whose first nucleus are Mary and the disciple Jesus loved.

This temple is open to all, as will shortly be demonstrated by the faith of a pagan centurion and the joining of other outsiders. The temple in Jerusalem, destroyed in 70 A.D., was never reconstructed. Even if it were, God would not dwell in it as before. Its time has ended. One era is over, another begins—the era of the fullness of grace.

*O Jesus, you are more alive after death than when you were living. I believe and I am happy that your love is victorious. I believe that death may be the greatest act of love. Help me to experience it in this manner.*

I must learn to look at my own and others' lives as God's most important dwelling place. I must respect sacred places, churches and holy images, but this must not prevent me from recognizing God's presence in the ordinary occurrences of history and in other people's lives.

## SCENE 17: GOD'S RESTORATION

It is not necessary to wait for the resurrection to realize that the Crucified is God. None of the evangelists postpone until then the reverberation felt throughout creation or the birth of faith in some of the onlookers. God's restoration, the answer of the Father to the cry of his Son, begins to take place as soon as his Son dies, while the echo of that cry is still in the air.

Moreover the cry itself, which in Mt and Mk is one with Jesus' last breath, is the touch that brings faith to life, as if to say that it will resound forever in humanity's ears, warning it not to reject God's love.

According to the Synoptics, the first fruit of Jesus' death is the faith of the Roman centurion who was in charge of the crucifixion. "When the centurion, who stood facing him, saw that he thus breathed his last, he said: 'Truly this man was the Son of God,'" Mk 15:39. For Mt, the same profession of faith is shared by "those who were with" the centurion, 27:54.

What has happened deep within the heart of these pagans? What did they see? All had seen the same thing, including the passersby and the high priests—a crucified man who dies crying aloud. They neither saw miracles nor observed him descending from the cross. And yet, the centurion saw God in this way of dying.

Death always reveals who we are. Jesus' death shows that he is God. Without faith one may die angry and rebellious, with faith death can be accepted in adoration and abandonment.

In his entire Gospel, Mk keeps Jesus' identity wrapped in mystery. But during his Passion Jesus accepted the titles which belong to him. Now they can be cried out at the top of one's voice, just as the dying Crucified cried out.

"Truly this man was the Son of God," Mt 27:54. Under the cross faith breaks out—it cannot be restrained. If the Jews reject it, the pagans proclaim it. It is folly, but it reveals God's secret.

In Lk, the centurion's declaration does not reach that same apex of faith. He only says: "Certainly this man was innocent!" 23:47. This can be explained by the fact that each evangelist wants to transmit a particular message to his community. Lk tries to convince the Romans that the Christian community is not a threat; in fact, their leader was declared innocent by both the procurator and by the centurion. The latter confirms that condemning him was a mistake.

Mt and Mk, on the contrary, must give strength to communities shaken by the fury of persecution. The persecution by Nero, in which Christians were fed to the lions or were crucified and set on fire to illuminate the roads, had perhaps already taken place in Rome. Repression was ferocious. Death is always frightening. But there, when all fails, you can surrender to God and testify that he is present and powerful, for he is your strength. For those who die in this manner, this is Gospel, the good news. The cross compels faith and nourishes it.

Besides the faith of the centurion, the Synoptics mention the faithfulness of the women who followed Jesus from Galilee, the same ones whom Jn presented beside the cross. It is said that these women observed from afar. Mt and Mk provide a list of names, making it clear that it is incomplete. They will also be present at Jesus' burial, thus preparing the reader for the surprise of the resurrection.

According to Lk, with the group of women are also "all those who had known him," 23:49. Who are they? They may be the disciples who, even keeping their distance, must have followed Jesus. As a matter of fact, Lk never mentioned their flight. Instead he stressed the effect of Jesus' prayer in the disciples' trials.

Still in Lk, "all the multitudes who assembled to see the sight, when they saw what had taken place, returned home beating their breasts," 23:48. He wants to demonstrate that there is always a crowd following Jesus, even in death. Not everyone is against him.

*O my Jesus, meditation on your Passion is always the most effective means of re-energizing faith. I want to keep close to this mystery, to grow in faith and love.*

St. Paul of the Cross says that "everything is encompassed in the Passion of Jesus"—all God's love, all of sin's ravaging power, all the forgiveness I need, all the example and strength to nourish my spiritual life. I must enrich my knowledge and my prayer by drawing from this source to invigorate my daily commitment.

## Scene 18: His heart speaks still

If everything has been accomplished nothing more should happen. Yet in Jn several symbolic occurrences of paramount importance follow. They do not come from nature nor from deep within the hearts of those present, but from the human body of the Crucified. With these Jn offers a first-hand theological interpretation of the meaning of Jesus' death.

The night draws near and the crucified bodies must disappear from public display. Shortly, the feast will begin and to touch them would cause legal impurity. Moreover, according to the Bible, they would fall under God's malediction, if they remained exposed during the night. The Jews, who unscrupulously had him killed, are now preoccupied with legal impurity, just as when for the same reason they did not want to enter the praetorium or to use the money returned by Judas. Therefore, they ask Pilate to order the soldiers to accelerate the death of the crucified men by breaking their legs.

The soldiers carry out the order. "But when they came to Jesus and saw that he was already dead, they did not break his legs. But one of the soldiers pierced his side with a spear and at once there came out blood and water," Jn 19:33-34.

It is the free decision of the officer. It is not for special treatment, but as an alternative assurance of death. The description of the scene is followed by a sentence in which Jn insists three times on the concept of witness. He saw it, therefore he tells the truth and we must believe him, cf. 19:35. The episode contains a cluster of four symbolic implications that summarize the meaning of Jesus' life, death and resurrection.

**The broken legs.** According to the ritual of the Hebrew Passover meal, no bones of the paschal lamb were to be broken, Ex 12:46 and Nb 9:12. In Jn, Jesus dies on the eve of Passover, while the lambs were being slaughtered in the temple. By not breaking his bones, the obvious implication is that he is the new paschal lamb.

**The pierced heart.** Its symbolism is one with the blood and water. It means that love has been given to the end, it has sacrificial and atoning significance that will never be extinguished.

**The blood.** It explains the theological sense of Jesus' death. Throughout the Bible blood indicates life, and blood poured out indicates death. But from the dead Jesus flows living blood. He is alive and he is the source from which springs the new life of the world. His pierced side is a doorway through which we may enter life, namely, intimate communion with Jesus' profound self-knowledge and identity.

Faith, love and doctrine have called this intimacy the "Heart" of Jesus. It expresses and summarizes Jesus' entire life, from birth to death and the resurrection. It is linked to the accomplishments of his mandate, to his love poured out to the very end.

**The water.** This represents the relationship between Jesus and the Holy Spirit after his death on the cross. It envisions the theology of the Holy Spirit. In Jn the Holy Spirit and Jesus are strictly united in the final phase of the work of salvation. Jesus "thirsts" to give his Spirit, he hands him over while breathing his last and, through the water flowing from his open heart, he confirms that the gift has been given.

As Jesus' life ends, the life of the Church begins. The blood sums up the past, the water holds the future: Jesus alive in history through the power of the Holy Spirit. The Church is born from his wounded heart.

Blood and water signify the salvific effects of Jesus' death, salvation taken as a whole, worked out by the Father, the Son and the Holy Spirit.

In harmony with the fruits of centuries of contemplation, it is legitimate to think that Jn alludes to the two main streams with which the Holy Spirit brings about salvation in the world: through baptism (water) and the Eucharist (blood).

*O my Jesus, your heart is our dwelling place. Only because you have enabled us to live in your heart, can we ourselves become the dwelling place of the Blessed Trinity.*

I have been baptized and have been receiving the Eucharist for many years. Is it possible to be nourished with these sources of energy without showing signs of growth in my conformity to Christ?

## SCENE 19: ALL EYES ARE UPON HIM

He promised to gather everyone around him. "When I am lifted up from the earth, I will draw all men to myself," Jn 12:32. They intended to lift him up on the cross so that everyone could mock him. For him, however, this was his exaltation at the top of the world for all to see and from where he can embrace the universe.

This is the "very high mountain," Mt 4:8, from which he can see the kingdoms of the world. Behold, now they are his. He did not conquer them with the violence of power which is always adoration of the devil, as Satan himself had proposed to him in the desert, but drew them to himself with the magnet of love.

"They shall look on him whom they have pierced," Jn 19:37; Zc 12:10. Jn ends his Passion narrative with this quotation from the prophet Zechariah that referred to death of the king of Jerusalem. His account began in 13:1 with this opening declaration at the washing of the feet: "When Jesus knew that his hour had come to depart out of this world to the Father, having loved his own who were in the world, he loved them to the end."

What he had anticipated with the washing of the feet and with the institution of the Eucharist he accomplished on Calvary.

The completion of his work consists not only in giving up his life for those he loved, but also in gathering them as the new people of God and pouring out upon them the gift of the Holy Spirit. He proclaimed that "all is finished," both in his words and with his open heart.

These words and gestures will be the foundation for the future development of every area of theology: Trinity, Christology, Pneumatology, Ecclesiology, Mariology, the Spiritual and Mystical Life.

The lifting up on the cross portrays the Crucified at the pinnacle of his glory. He is the "Lord" of a new people—the Christian community. The power of the resurrection is not severed from the power of the cross. To say that "God is love" is not enough. It could merely be a beautiful philosophy or perhaps theology. It is necessary to add that love emptied itself and has been poured out upon us. This is the God of Jesus Christ, revealed on the cross.

We will never stop looking towards the one whom they have pierced. Who, according to Jn, is gazing at the Crucified? Is it the mother and the disciple? He does not specify. Is it his enemies and the soldiers? It is not likely. These must already have left Calvary.

It is probable that Jn is describing the sentiment of faith which is born around the Crucified, thanks to the blood and water flowing from his open heart. Those who gaze upon the Crucified are the witnesses of faith down through the centuries, beginning with those present at the foot of the cross until the Crucified will appear again in all his glory at the end of time.

To gaze upon the Crucified means to draw faith and be transformed by him and to witness to him so that the entire world will be transformed. Whoever looks with faith at the open-hearted Crucified will understand God's love and be overwhelmed by it.

To see, to look, to comprehend are the verbs used by Jn to indicate the experience of faith. Faith may entail suffering as in the case of our Lady of Sorrows or Mary Magdalene, but it will bring salvation. He who looks at the Crucified will understand that "He is," that he is God, and will be saved.

The silent flow of blood and water is the ultimate revelation of God.

In capsule form, who pierced him? The Jewish and Roman leaders, Israel, humanity, you and me. Who looks at him? All can. His mother, the perfect disciple, the women from near and from afar, the crowd of people striking their breasts are the first. All the saved of all times follow. Now, it is you and I who cannot turn our eyes away from him. Think of the ecstasy of St. Paul of the Cross, his head on the open heart of Jesus.

*O Jesus, there is no scene more powerful than this—you, lifted up on the cross with your open heart. May my eyes and heart never cease looking at you.*

I cannot look at the Crucified and remain on the margins of Christian commitment. It is a dynamic gaze. It means to follow, to imitate, to give up one's life like him—"in memory of him," as it is said in the Eucharist.

## SCENE 20: THE FULL TOMB

Dying is not only breathing one's last but also ending up in a tomb. There, death brings its victory to completion by destroying our body. After sharing our death, Jesus also experiences our tomb.

The evangelists recount his burial with an abundance of details, to leave no doubt that he really died and to prepare the emotional reaction to the resurrection.

The job is performed hastily. The ritual anointing of the corpse is omitted because it is late and because Jesus had already been anointed at Bethany. Moreover a pretext must be left for the women to come back and anoint him after the feast.

Jn tells us that Jesus was covered with one hundred pounds of myrrh and aloes. This was not the usual ritual anointing of the dead but a sign of honor. When Herod the Great died, he was dipped in several hundred pounds of just such fragrant mixtures. This treatment bestowed upon Jesus speaks of a royal burial, but it also tells us that no expectation of the resurrection was in the air.

A new figure appears on the scene, Joseph of Arimathea. He is a good and righteous man, until now an anonymous disciple of Jesus, who was longing for the kingdom of God, like the prophet Simeon. He is from Judea, and, together with the women who came from Galilee and the centurion from pagan Rome, this completes the geographical profile of Jesus' followers.

Joseph is a distinguished member of the Sanhedrin, and this clearly shows that not even the leaders of the nation were unanimous in rejecting Jesus. He is rich, thus demonstrating that the Christian community does not turn its back on the wealthy who put themselves out for Jesus. He is courageous because he takes a real risk by becoming involved with one who was condemned by the official authority.

He asks Pilate's permission to take away Jesus' body. The word used is not cadaver but body, the same term used for the Eucharist. The bodies of the executed were thrown into the common graves, but family members could request them. The Roman procurator consents to the wish, surprised not so much by the interest of one of the Jewish leaders, but by the suddenness of Jesus' death.

Along with Joseph of Arimathea, Jn mentions Nicodemus who had already appeared twice in his Gospel. He also is one of the leaders. Up to this moment he did not have the courage to follow Jesus by openly taking a position against the judgment of his colleagues, but the events of Calvary gave him the strength to come out of hiding and take a risk for Jesus.

The burial is carried out with great reverence despite the lack of time. Jesus is taken down from the cross, bound in white linen cloths and placed in a new tomb carved in the rock. It was the tomb that Joseph of Arimathea had prepared for himself, one in which no one had ever been laid. The entrance is blocked by a stone that would be difficult to move.

The Synoptics call our attention to the presence of the women during the burial. Lk points out that they are those who came from Galilee, faithful disciples as usual. They "saw the tomb and how his body was laid," 23:55. They must return later to complete the work, therefore, they need to understand how to handle the dead body. Mt names Mary Magdalene and her friend. They are strong, while the male disciples are weak and absent.

165

Faith and devotion have always considered it only logical that at the time of the burial ceremony Jesus' body would have at some time been placed in the arms of his mother Mary before being handed over to mother earth. We cannot find confirmation of this in the Gospel, but his mother is there and the scene of the "Pietà" is a legitimate source of meditation and of artistic expression.

According to Jn the burial takes place in a garden. Is there a connection with the garden of Gethsemane? Or is there a relationship with the garden of Eden, where the human adventure began? In fact, a new creation is going to explode here with the resurrection of Jesus.

Everything in this scene leaves the impression of a temporary arrangement. It will not last.

*O my Jesus, welcome to the city of the dead, where countless human beings dwell already and where all are journeying. Knowing that you were there makes it easier to accept that our destination is there as well.*

The other world is one of life's most disquieting problems. Why does everything seem to go on just as it always had after Jesus' death and resurrection? Why can't someone render us tranquil by explaining how things really stand in the world beyond? The obscurity of faith lasts to the end. Many cannot endure not knowing and resort to the occult and to paranormal and magic powers. Faith helps me to accept my destiny without useless turmoil to avoid it.

SCENE 21: THE USELESS GUARD

Hours of silence and suspense follow the burial. Around the isolated tomb an atmosphere of expectation and fear are almost palpable. The hurried burial left the impression of incompleteness. The heavy stone that had been rolled in front of the tomb seems an exaggeration for the custody of the dead.

The women have taken note of even the smallest of details because they must return to finish the job. In reality, we do not know if they left or remained there. Mt says: "Mary Magdalene and the other Mary were there, sitting opposite the sepulcher," 27:61. Maybe they took turns for the wake.

Mt adds a tragicomic ingredient to these elements of apprehension. The day of the Passover, the Jewish leaders go to Pilate and ask him to order that the sepulcher be made secure for at least three days. "Sir, we remember how that impostor said while he was still alive: 'After three days I will rise again,'" 27:63. It is necessary to keep watch, otherwise his fanatic supporters will take him away and tell the people that he rose from the dead.

Pilate, who is fed up with them and with the whole matter, roughly dismisses them and tells them to use their own guards. He has no intention of shaming the Roman army by commanding them to keep watch over a dead Jew. So, "They went and made the sepulcher secure by sealing the stone and setting a guard," 27:66.

Mt uses the incident to emphasize the fact that their rejection of Jesus is so obstinate that it pursues him even to the grave. Their antagonism drives them to lose their sense of dignity.

The irony fairly crackles in the unfolding of the account. The drama ends forcing Jesus' enemies to declare the truth. Yesterday, Pilate had condemned Jesus after declaring that he was innocent. Today, he allows the Jews to set a guard before the tomb, after they admit their concern that Jesus would indeed rise from the dead. They feared him when he was alive and they are afraid of him now that he is dead.

This is meant to be a warning for Mt's community: the difficulties they are facing are no different than those of Jesus.

Mt likes contrasts. By the tomb there are now two escorts: one of love expressed by the women who with hope keep vigil; one of rejection expressed by the Jewish guards who do not want to give in to the Nazarene.

The Passion ends just as it had begun: a woman anointed

him with love while his enemies plotted against him. Now several women are there, strong in their following of Jesus, while his enemies are there stubborn to the end in their rejection. It is always a matter of love and hatred, hope and mistrust, fellowship and rejection, right and wrong choices. It is the everlasting drama of the world before the Crucified.

Even from the tomb Jesus continues to teach. The agitation that follows his crucifixion shows that he is still alive and active. He is no longer among the living, he cannot be seen and cannot be heard. It seems that he no longer exists, and yet he is saving the world as he did on the cross.

The Christian experience must also take into account the spirituality of the sepulcher. Life does not only consist of appearance and success. Sooner or later the moment comes in which only silence and loneliness remain. We must learn to accept them with love. They can be more fruitful and constructive than most externally visible accomplishments.

Jesus not only taught and died to save the world, but he also went down into the sepulcher. It may not always be necessary to perform generous actions in order to do good before God. We may also be called to disappear into the sepulcher.

*O Jesus, in the sepulcher you are as alive as on the cross. So much so that even there you are at the center of love and rejection. Help me to love you even in that supreme silence in which nothingness and entirety meet.*

We are naturally attracted to the spotlight and center stage. Today, the culture of the catwalk, the microphone and celebrity has taken over. We cannot live without at least a small group of followers. We must learn to appreciate the silence of loneliness and of the sepulcher, and visit and keep company with those who find themselves in such conditions.

# III. THE EPILOGUE

Mt 28     Mk 16     Lk 24     Jn 20 and 21

## SCENE 1: THE EMPTY TOMB

**Reflect.** From the manner in which the evangelists recount Jesus' death and burial it is clear that he would be resurrected. The new era coincides with Jesus' death and is manifested by unmistakable signs: the tearing of the veil of the temple, the cosmic quakes which reveal the presence of God, the proclamation of the divine identity of the Crucified, the conversions, the blood and water from the pierced heart.

But the evangelists understood all this only after the resurrection. This is why they do not end their Gospel with the death and burial, but report also the historic events that are the foundation of faith and of the Christian testimony to the resurrection of Jesus. These events are: the empty tomb, the apparitions of the risen Lord and the transformation of the disciples.

The historical event of Jesus' passage from death to life cannot be recounted because no one saw it and because it is a divine action that can only be perceived by faith. The historical elements of the empty tomb and of the apparitions are reported and transmitted to us as testimonies which, if accepted, open us to the gift of faith.

For Mk the empty tomb is sufficient to attest that Jesus is risen. It is not necessary to see him alive. The women who on the first day after the Sabbath arrive with perfumes to anoint Jesus' body find that the stone has been rolled away and that the tomb is empty. A young man dressed in white waits for them and announces: "He has risen, he is not here," 16:6. Then he orders them to tell the disciples to gather in Galilee to meet Jesus as promised. But no encounter with Jesus is reported. Thus Mk's Gospel ends. Another hand added the subsequent passages to mention the apparitions narrated by the other evangelists.

The first events give rise to astonishment but not to faith. Those who first hear about the empty tomb remain puzzled. Unexpected messengers say that he is risen—a man in Mk, two in Lk, an angel in Mt. But they are not convincing. The resurrection is beyond anyone's expectation.

In Mt the tomb breaks open in the presence of the women just arrived on the spot and is accompanied by an earthquake similar to the one that took place at Jesus' death on the cross. The women are reassured by the angel and sent to bring the news to the disciples.

The stunned guards rush to report the fact to their leaders and are paid to spread the version that the disciples have stolen the body with violence. The corruption of power is not only an issue of our days!

According to Lk and Jn the women run to inform the apostles, but these think that they are hallucinating.

In all of the Gospel narratives Mary Magdalene is personally involved. In Jn she is alone when she discovers the open tomb. She hastily departs to inform Peter and the disciple loved by Jesus. Only the latter believes after seeing the empty tomb. Perhaps he noticed that the linen shroud in which the body had been wrapped was lying on the ground emptied of the body but not unraveled—this may have helped him believe.

The tomb is empty—this is evident. But faith is still difficult, both for those who love like Mary Magdalene and for those who feel the need to rationalize, like Peter.

**Pray.** *O Jesus, teach me where to look for you. Give me the ability to perceive your presence in events and in people.*

**Promise.** What prevents me from encountering the risen Christ is the pretension that he must manifest himself according to my ways instead of his. My effort to adapt my thinking to God's mind must last a lifetime. I cannot celebrate the resurrection of Jesus from the tomb without witnessing it in my own life.

## SCENE 2: HE IS ALIVE!

The empty tomb does not succeed in stripping away the disbelief and the discouragement into which the hurricane of the Passion had thrown the disciples. Therefore, behold the apparitions.

They do not occur with the dazzling light of fireworks, but in a simple and familial way, along the roads, in the workplace, during meals. They do not aim to crush the opponents and eliminate all obstacles, but to consolidate the faith so that it can become the foundation for faith's future. The Risen Lord does not show off before the Roman emperor or those who had rejected him, but he goes to meet the humble ones who had followed him and had been disheartened by the apparent failure of the Passion.

Mt recounts two apparitions—to the women at the sepulcher and to the disciples in Galilee. The women obey the angel's request and go to bring the news to the apostles. The apostles see the Risen One while they are still secluded for fear of the Jews. "Jesus met them and said: 'Hail!'" 28:9. He confirms that their mission is to go and announce the good news. The apparition teaches that fidelity is rewarded and that Jesus always reaches his disciples and remains with them when they are on their mission. In Galilee the promised encounter takes place—along with the restoration of relationships and faith. It ends by Jesus sending the disciples forth to "make disciples of all nations," 28:19.

Lk describes three apparitions: to the disciples at Emmaus, to the community in Jerusalem, and the final encounter "out as far as Bethany," 24:50, when he was carried up into heaven.

Jn reports the largest number of apparitions of the Risen One—his focus is not Jesus but the transformation of the disciples. For him it is useless to insist on the resurrection. That is obvious from the narration of the Passion. He narrates four cases that are unforgettable expressions of the power of faith in transforming human beings: the encounter with Mary Magdalene, with all the disciples except Thomas, with the disciples including Thomas, with the disciples on the lakeshore.

Mary Magdalene, who at first glance thinks he is the gardener, transforms her ardent love into missionary commitment, to the point of becoming "the apostle of the apostles" (John Paul II).

The very day of the resurrection Jesus reaches the disciples who are barricaded at home, and bestows upon them the gift of the Holy Spirit already poured out from the cross. Those who were frightened are now aglow with joy.

One week later Jesus reappears to catch Thomas, who has had problems with faith, also in the group. He too is transformed. The sight of the Risen Lord elicits from his lips the most beautiful profession of faith ever uttered: "My Lord and my God!" 20:28. In turn, his profession of faith puts on Jesus' lips the most beautiful beatitude he ever pronounced: "Blessed are those who have not seen and yet believe," 20:29.

Before ascending to heaven Jesus let himself be seen again by the sea of Tiberias. Perhaps the disciples are disillusioned. They have gone back to their previous jobs. It must be the crisis of ordinary life and routine. Or maybe in the community there are concerns over the different roles of Peter and John. Three times Peter affirms his love for Jesus, counterbalancing his threefold denial during the Passion. As far as John's function is concerned, everyone must answer his own calling and accomplish his own mission. You "follow me," 21:19.

Almost all of the apparitions have common elements: the disciples doubt, they believe they see a ghost, they are not excited. It is impossible to infer that they invented the facts or were hallucinating.

Jesus rebukes them for their incredulity, he stirs up their faith, he lets himself be recognized and touched, he recalls their past life together, he partakes in their meals. Often they recognize him in the "breaking of the bread" that is, in the celebration of the Eucharist. The ultimate touch of his infinite gentleness is that he never scolds them for their failure during the Passion.

The Risen Lord remains with his own for as long as it is necessary to guarantee that their faith is strong enough to resist in time of trial and to be transmitted.

*O Jesus, risen and alive, grant that faith in the resurrection transform my life as it transformed the lives of the apostles.*

Faith in the resurrection is a gift with countless consequences. It can never be appreciated enough. It can only be received and assimilated with great humility. Often resurrection is something totally different from what we think it is. I must ask God to grow in the experience of this mystery.

SCENE 3: HE IS WITH US

How many times did the Risen Lord appear? Between those recounted by the evangelists and those listed by the apostle Paul in 1 Cor 15:5-8, it is likely that Jesus appeared on at least a dozen occasions, to different individuals and groups, including one apparition to "more than five hundred brethren at one time." But we are not sure that all of the apparitions have been reported.

Given that each author mentions only the ones he considers important for his purpose, we may assume that many others have not been handed down to us. At the end of his book on the "Exercises" St. Ignatius of Loyola proposes a "way of light" with the same scheme as the "way of the cross" in which he retraces fourteen apparitions.

No one speaks of a special apparition of the Risen Jesus to

his mother Mary. Is it possible that he manifested himself to Mary Magdalene and not to his mother? One rich Church tradition considers it obvious that such an apparition must certainly have occurred.

In such a case however, it would have had a completely different purpose. All the apparitions reported in the Gospels intend to give foundation to faith and to confirm it—which Mary did not need since her faith never vacillated. But if we consider the emotional mother-son relationship, which the Incarnate Word valued so highly, such an apparition is very likely. Moreover it is logical that Mary saw her Risen Son when he showed himself to his apostles and other followers.

How long did Jesus stay with his community after the resurrection, before the ascension into heaven? The forty days mentioned in the Scriptures signify a perfect period of time, that is the time necessary for the faith of the witnesses to be so strong as to be the foundation and support of faith in centuries to come.

Lk recounts the ascension of Jesus twice, at the end of his Gospel and at the beginning of the Acts of the Apostles. In the first case the ascension takes place the same day of the resurrection, in the second forty days after. In the first case he intends to link the ascension with the resurrection, in the second with the descent of the Holy Spirit. The Risen Lord took all the time he deemed necessary to set in motion a journey that no one can ever stop.

What does the resurrection mean?

*For the Father* it means that he listened to his Son and proclaims that he is right. Since the resurrection is a historical event, by raising his Son from death the Father pronounces in history a judgment against history. The judgment of history, under the influence of sin, was to eliminate Jesus. There was no place for a life only motivated by love in a world possessed by sin. With the resurrection, the Father eliminates this pronouncement of history and affirms that it has been an immense mistake. Through the power of the Holy Spirit, the Father relaunches the Son into history to make possible in it an authentic model of human life, the only one corresponding to the original plan of creation.

*For the Son* the resurrection entails entering into the glory of the Father also with his human nature but glorified by the resurrection and still bearing the signs of his Passion. Moreover, it entails reentering human history no longer as Jesus of Nazareth but as the Paschal Jesus who has become the Vivifying Spirit. To his new life he joins the new community of the believers. His glorious body is also his mystical body extended and prolonged in humanity, in which he brings about human salvation through the word and the sacraments.

*For us* the resurrection means to grow in the new life of Jesus received in baptism and through faith, and nourished every Sunday in the Lord's Supper. From there we draw strength to live, giving up our lives out of love for the transformation of the world. In the Eucharist we encounter the Risen Lord who gathers us as he did the disciples in Galilee. He remains with us, fortifying us with his word and the breaking of the bread so that our energies will not diminish.

Finally the resurrection means that we will also share Jesus' condition to the extent that it is possible for human nature, after this life and at the end of time.

*O my Jesus, thank you for sharing your life with me. The Christian life, after all, means the life of the Risen Lord. For this reason, living, suffering and dying in love means to experience the power of the resurrection.*

Whatever in my life is against Jesus or rejects Jesus has already been judged as wrong by the Father in raising Jesus from the dead. Only what conforms to Christ has validity. Anything else can turn against me. My spiritual life must be open to the Father so that he may accomplish in me his plan of making the Risen Lord the heart of the world.

"Resurrezione"

# Main Features of the Crucified Christ According to Each Evangelist

*In every Passion narrative the image of Jesus corresponds to the presentation given by each evangelist in the rest of his Gospel. This is true in every passage of the account right up until his death.*

*We have already seen this in our meditations, but we would like to focus once again on this aspect from a bird's eye view. Just as artists express the different features of the Crucified with colors, marble, words or musical notes, we propose to do the same with our contemplative reflections.*

*They will consist of retrospective glances, laden with trepidation and humility, since it is a matter of capturing traits of the heart more than those of the face. The aim is to impress them within our hearts, not to produce a work of art.*

*Remember that the Passion narratives of Mt and Mk are considered twin accounts since they present analogous characteristics of the Crucified. Mt has a more refined style, clearly situating the events in the light of the Old Testament while reporting additional details.*

*No one should be surprised if a trait emphasized by one evangelist can also be found in others.*

# I. MATTHEW

### 1. FULFILLED THROUGH OBEDIENCE

**Reflect**. Obedience out of love is fulfilling while a forced obedience is oppressive. In giving his life Jesus obeys the will of the Father, who does not want his Son's death, but the salvation of the world.

It does not make sense to say that the Father is merciless. He saved Isaac from Abraham's dagger and the three children from the fiery furnace, but he did not save his Son from the cross. The Father so loves the world that he gives his Son. The Son lives in the Father's love and exists because he is the Father's gift. Also as man he reaches fulfillment insofar as he is generated by the Father's love.

As man he freely decides that the best way to save the world is to give up his own life out of love. Thus he fulfills at the same time the will of the Father, the work of salvation and the realization of himself. He would never accept not to die since he understood that this was the only way of expressing, in human terms, God's love.

The *Catechism of the Catholic Church* summarizes his accomplishments: By his obedience unto death, Jesus accomplished the substitution of the Suffering Servant, who "makes himself an *offering for sin*," when "he bore the sin of many," and who "shall make many to be accounted righteous," for "he shall bear their iniquities. Jesus atoned for our faults and made satisfaction for our sins to the Father," 615.

Since the beginning of his ministry, Mt's Jesus makes it clear that he must "fulfill all righteousness." This is what he says to John the Baptist who hesitated when Jesus asked to be baptized. Righteousness means a right thing to be accomplished, for it derives from God's plan and expresses his will. In this case it is the salvation of humanity which will be brought about on the cross.

No one can stop Jesus from accomplishing it. The devil is the first to set roadblocks with the temptations in the desert. Jesus' own disciples try to hold him back, especially Peter. His opponents uselessly attempt to stop him.

During the Passion, Jesus' intention becomes progressively clearer. He enters into the Paschal Supper declaring it his "hour" —that is, the final hour and the time for everything to be accomplished. To the bread and wine of the Supper Jesus confers the meaning of his death and bestows upon them his permanent presence within the community. This is not just any death, but a death freely chosen out of love.

While the disciples are sleeping, he experiences the agony of one who desires God's will and adheres to it, thus standing out as the model of perfect prayer. When he is arrested he refuses violence in his defense. Before the leaders of his people he confesses his identity as Son of God and his mission as savior, while Peter denies his own identity as disciple. For this, Jesus is rejected and covered with insults. The same occurs before the Roman authorities.

His faithfulness to God contrasts sharply with the infidelity of the people, who choose Barabbas, a murderer, rather than the true king of Israel. On the cross, tempted in his solitude, pursued by insults and challenged to come down, he remains faithful to the Father and in the midst of pain hands his life over to him. Yet through his final cry and the promptness of his obedient love he feels fulfilled.

While the leaders of Israel fail because by rejecting him they reject the promised Messiah, Jesus succeeds because he remains faithful to the Father. Thus he fulfills salvation for humanity, including Israel if it wants to accept it.

**Pray.** *O my Jesus, your obedience is the fruit of your freedom and it results in my liberation. Your freedom is invested and spent* *with one goal: the will of the Father and the salvation of the world. It means to live for love and to bend only to the power of love. Help me to use my freedom for good, not to consume it for nothing.*

**Promise.** Obedience has religious and salvific value insofar as it accepts the will of God in the concrete circumstances of life. Am I capable of linking my life, on a daily basis, with this plan of love and to answer it with love?

## 2. THE VICTORY OF THE VANQUISHED

In the Passion the more values are denied the more they are affirmed. The more Jesus is made a slave the more he reigns. The more he is rejected the more he counts and is accepted. The more they want to take away or deny—his dignity, respect, acceptance, his very life—the more Jesus receives, to the resurrection.

He is rejected not only generically but in a "scientific" manner, with the demolition of his personality, point by point.

He is rejected as the Christ, God's anointed one, the Messiah king and liberator. By accepting this rejection with love, he fulfills his rejected task. He frees us as he is being rejected as liberator.

He is repudiated as Son of Man and as Son of God; as king of Israel by the Jews and as king of the Jews by the pagans. Yet, while they reject these titles they affirm that they are true, otherwise why would they oppose them so ferociously?

"It is you who say it," Jesus says to the high priest and to Pilate who question him about these titles. Indeed, "you will see the Son of Man seated at the right hand of the power, and coming on the clouds of heaven." The derision and the rejection follow him to the cross, but even there an unsuspected witness, the pagan centurion, proclaims that he is the Son of God. The more he appears weak and defeated in human terms, the more he appears strong and a winner according to God and in faith's understanding.

The same can be said for human values. He is betrayed by one friend, denied by another, condemned by the authorities and by the people. To betray, to deny, to abandon, to condemn are the four fundamental verbs in the distortion of human relationships. They include all the wrong and sinful actions of this area: misunderstandings, suspicions, incommunicability, dampening of sentiments, indifference, falseness of heart, mistrust, gossip, accusations, manipulations, rejection, insults, calumny, hatred, homicides.

Jesus assumes and shares with love these human experiences. In a certain way, he places himself right in the middle of them, so that any human being who faces them will encounter him.

At the same time though, he denounces the injustice of those who treat their neighbors in such a manner, and he announces that human dignity is not destroyed, on the contrary it is strengthened in those who are submitted to such abuse.

He accepts to be betrayed, arrested, stripped, scourged, crowned with thorns, insulted, condemned to death, to express to what extent it is possible to love, but also to shout out that no one has the right to treat another human being in such a manner. One who is subject to this treatment must know that he loses nothing, because God is close by, and because no one can strip another of his or her human dignity. In fact, the one who inflicts such torture on another reduces his own dignity in the process.

It is not the person who is offended who is degraded, but the one who offends. He who insults, insults himself and he who kills suppresses his own human dignity. This is the message of the Passion even in its most basic aspect.

The Passion is the celebration of human values and of life itself, even if it ends with death on the cross.

The power abused to destroy Jesus is itself destroyed by

the only power which counts: love which gives life, carried out during the Passion and on the cross. True power does not consist in making others die, but in dying for others. It comes from God and it means to serve. To serve is to reign.

*O my Jesus, your cross is the most amazing revelation of God, a God who does not remain aloof but who comes down and fills our life with meaning, above all in its obscure aspects in which, on our own, we cannot find meaning.*

Christ accepted crucifixion to give meaning to all crosses, but also to denounce those who crucify others. I must evaluate my relationship with others—do I exploit the cross, force it upon others, unload it on others and compel them to carry it?

### 3. A DEAD MAN WHO LIVES

The abuse of power maneuvered by sin is responsible for the death of Jesus on the cross. As soon as the Crucified dies, Mt describes the signs of life. He cannot wait for the forty or so hours that Jesus is enclosed in the tomb.

It is not necessary to await the resurrection to become aware of the vitality of the Crucified. The proclamation of divinity made by the centurion poses a worrisome question—what will become of that crucified man? He did not die a normal death. It is a death with a message, intended to prove an argument. All appealed to his power, challenging him to come down from the cross. If he can destroy the temple and rebuild it in three days, if he is the Son of God, if he has saved others—then surely he can free himself from this situation.

Of course he could have, but he did not. He could have revealed himself as they had asked of him; instead he revealed himself as he chose to, so much so that someone noticed it. How can this be explained?

He could have freed himself from the cross with a miracle

or with an extraordinary technical-scientific intervention. For example, he could have had himself lifted off by a spaceship or with the explosion of an atomic bomb which would have destroyed all of Jerusalem and a large part of Judea. But in such a manner he would have stolen our allegiance. We would have had to admit that he was right, but without faith or love. He would have lowered himself to our level by competing with us for the spectacular. We would have been capable of the same feats some twenty centuries later. He would have stupefied the Jews who look for miracles and the Greeks who appreciate logic. But the effectiveness of the "sign" would have dissipated with time.

Thus, in waiting for the resurrection, what sign was there that he is God? The sign is this: remaining on the cross. They asked him to give them a sign by descending; he gave them a sign by not descending. By coming down from the cross he would have given a sign of power; by not coming down he gave a sign of love.

If he would have given us a sign of power he would have been playing our game and we would have compared ourselves to him and justified our manias of being gods ourselves. By giving us a sign of love he presented us with a challenge which we will never be able to reach. Twenty centuries later we are still hobbling from our precipices in an attempt to imitate him, like an insect that cannot climb out of a glass jar.

What would we have done with a God who would have come down from his cross, when we cannot leave our crosses but must carry them and die with them? In this manner the Crucified is close to our crosses. He is always with us. He is each of us. This is one of the most powerful and energizing points in the contemplation of the Crucified. He is so human that we understand him. He is so divine that it is impossible to reach him, even though it is always possible to approach him.

He is the simple and arduous "beyond" which attracts us and flees from us, which provokes and challenges us. In spite of all the progress of our intelligence, of our science and of our technology we remain distant. Only saints come close. Only on that path can we resemble God.

There are two "beyonds" to which the Crucified calls and attracts us: the beyond of love to the end on the cross and the beyond of the empty tomb. Both are a folly and a scandal. They overcome and surpass all human ways, thus they reveal God. Thus God is there.

*We adore you, O Christ, and we praise you, because by your holy cross you have redeemed the world.*

Today our technological and scientific progress have reached great heights, but spiritually we are regressing, we are at a standstill or we have gone back centuries. This is caused in large part by our rejection of the wisdom of the cross. The wisdom of the cross is part of the structure of the human spirit. Without it, it is impossible to overcome limits and to find meaning in everything. I must understand it and be witness to it.

## 4. The Crucified, a relationship to be resolved

The death of Jesus on the cross cannot be an insignificant event in history. Humanity now revolves around the Crucified.

The winners lose just as they abandon themselves to the euphoria of victory.

Opposition runs through the whole Gospel of Mt, as it does the others, and breaks into a furious crescendo in the Passion. Opposition gathers for a final conspiracy while Jesus is at supper with his friends in Bethany. It makes a pact with Judas, then gets rid of him when he is consumed with remorse. It hurls itself against Jesus, arresting him with a useless display of violence. It weaves false testimony into the religious trial, and it manipulates Pilate and the crowd in the civil trial. It covers Jesus with insults and incivilities, and it prefers the liberation of an assassin. It pursues the Crucified with derision and provocations even at the cross. It positions the guards and has the tomb sealed. Even after death the rejection of Jesus continues, as if in reply to a love which death has made inextinguishable.

A love to the end is responded to with a refusal to the end. But only the end of love is endless.

There is nothing that can be done. All the efforts of the opponents fail. Mt transmits to his community and to readers of all time a severe warning: opposition to Jesus is destined to fail. Before the Gospel and the Crucified we are all invited to resolve our responsibility positively.

Followers of Jesus can never consider themselves safe. Before the cross the crisis is so great that they collapse. In Mt their faith is weak. In Mk they are without faith. It is disconcerting but it is not kept silent.

At the supper in Bethany they complain about the perfume which is wasted on Jesus. The Passover meal is saddened by predictions of scandal, abandonment, betrayal and denial. In Gethsemane they sleep while Jesus prays and tries to involve them in prayer. At his arrest they awkwardly try using the sword, then they all flee. Peter follows at a distance but then ruins his fidelity to Jesus and his own dignity. Mt follows Judas to the end without compassion, a warning to the disciples that everyone can fail.

The coming together of the disciples in Galilee, the confirmation of trust and their being sent out into the world as missionaries bring the relationship between them and Jesus to a positive conclusion, yet the warning remains severe and inexorable. Even the closest of his followers, on their own, cannot accomplish much.

The weakness of faith leaves an indelible mark on Jesus' community. There is never enough faith. It is stupendous to follow Jesus, but it is not easy. We cannot fool ourselves by counting on our own strength. Persecution, physical and moral suffering and above all death are instances where faith is tested to the utmost and its scarcity comes to light. It is not possible to endure life's great crosses if we cannot embrace the daily ones.

It is possible that those who appear to be outsiders surpass those who consider themselves closest to Jesus. This theme is present from Mt's first pages. The Magi, the centurion of Capernaum, the Canaanite woman, the sinners who follow Jesus wherever he may go although the leaders oppose him, foretell that salvation is not similar to the right to free assistance, but involves the responsibility of each individual.

Five cases confirm this also in the Passion. The unknown woman from Bethany senses that Jesus is about to die while his followers criticize her initiative. Pilate's pagan wife defines Jesus as an innocent man. Beneath the cross only a few women tremble and only the centurion and his soldiers believe. One of the crucified criminals is admitted into paradise. For the burial, Joseph of Arimathea comes forward unexpectedly, at the last minute.

Before the Crucified each one must exercise his or her own freedom—without making a mistake.

*O my Jesus, your love is also for me. It calls me even when I do not feel like paying attention to it. Sometimes my weakness seems without end, but only your love is without end. I must abandon myself to your love.*

What position do I take before the Crucified? Am I among those who oppose him? If so what do I gain from remaining a failure? If I am among his disciples, how strong is my faith? If I am among the strangers or the indifferent, why do I not become involved?

188

# II. MARK

## 1. DEATH AS A RESULT OF LIFE

**Reflect.** The life and death of Jesus are strictly interdependent. Mk begins his Gospel with Jesus' ministry. The first conspiracy appears in 3:6, after only five actions of Jesus—between miracles or teachings considered intolerable by his opponents. "The Pharisees went out and immediately held counsel with the Herodians against him, how to destroy him."

Jesus is not obsessed by a suicidal vocation, but he is impassioned by the Father's kingdom. He wants to restore it because it has been interfered with and defaced by sin. He does not choose death, but he does choose to announce the kingdom. Acceptance of the kingdom requires a change of heart and a change in the social structures where they do not conform to God's plan; thus Jesus will be rejected. Death is neither desired nor searched out, but it is included as a consequence of the reaction to the plan. Thus, it is foreseen. If Jesus would change the message he would not be rejected, but this would leave the world as it is, at the mercy of the uncontested forces of evil. If he does not announce the kingdom he does not accomplish the mission for which he came—this is unthinkable.

Jesus is not forced to his Passion and death but lives for them. The Passion is not accidental, but is one of the events included in the Father's plan. The carrying of the cross acquires the meaning of a taking "the cross upon himself" and moving forward. It is not mere "tolerance" of the cross. In the end, to take the cross upon oneself becomes the definition both of the life and the mission of Jesus and his followers.

In Mk's narrative the Passion evolves along with a cluster of events which as they unfold reveal the mystery. The two ini-

189

tial suppers speak of death and offer details of its meaning. In Bethany, an anonymous woman disciple pours expensive perfume on Jesus' head foreshadowing Jesus' imminent death and the ritual anointment. In the cenacle, the Passover meal prefigures the universal meal with which Jesus will nourish all humanity—his body and his blood. Meanwhile Judas and the Sanhedrin have already contracted to betray him. Moral solitude becomes physical loneliness also when in Gethsemane Jesus is abandoned into the hands of his adversaries.

Before the Sanhedrin he reveals, without further hesitation, his identity by answering the questions which had been left hanging throughout the Gospel. However, as soon as he reveals his identity he is rejected by the people and denied by one of his disciples. To the Roman authorities he only responds with a sharp "You are the one who is saying it." Then he keeps silent until he cries out at his death. Only on the cross is the revelation of his identity and of his intent clearly disclosed.

None of the evangelists uses theological concepts or reasoning. They speak only through gestures and symbols. Mk is the driest of all. He does not even refer to the motivation of love. Jesus moves forward, faithful to the Father, to himself and to his mission, without surrendering to his emotions. And yet, his death speaks of love with the same effectiveness. Power dominated by sin, in order to remain coherent within itself must eliminate the Righteous One who lives for love.

Since the principle of the cross entails love to the end, it will always be rejected wherever sin dominates. No society can seriously believe that love can become a charter of its structure. The "civilization of love" or the "witness of charity" proposed by the Church can become reality only in the measure in which they are confirmed by the cross.

Jesus was considered an outlaw, and thus condemned according to the law.

**Pray.** *O my Jesus, the presence of sin has polluted everything, yet the strength of love can purify all. But this love is called "cross" and "cross" means life spent for others.*

**Promise**. Asserting the centrality of the cross must not be reduced to rhetoric or to philosophy. It means to call upon the example offered by Jesus, possibly witnessed by our efforts to follow him. By virtue of this relationship with Jesus, my life must show that only consuming oneself out of love can be fulfilling. Thus love becomes cross, which in turn eliminates crosses and uplifts the crucified of the world.

## 2. DEATH AS A CRY TO GOD

Death fully reveals Jesus' identity. He is the Son of God. Yet in Mk Jesus dies the poorest and most miserable death imaginable. How is it possible that such a death can manifest the divinity? The answer is this: giving his life up for others reveals the messianic identity of Jesus. But this is a theological elaboration derived from the spare account of the evangelist.

He writes with biblical images in mind: the Servant of God, the Righteous One of Israel, the Son of Man. All these images are human, subject to pain and to death, yet they do not exclude flashes of the divine. With these images Mk can paint Jesus' death with the darkest hues of a human death but still leave flashes of light which hint at his divine identity.

Love has taken Jesus to the bleakest possible state in human experience. No human being can find himself in a worse situation: physical pain, and worse still solitude and abandonment. It is almost a nullification. Even the Father seems to have disappeared. The divine light appears to have gone out. Jesus touches that kind of reduction to nothing that every human being must experience when he consciously brushes up against death. Jesus stands in man's abyss and there he lingers so that no man, even as he falls into it, feels alone.

Having descended to the very bottom, nothing of the human experience remains unknown to him. No one understands human life like he does. Only he knows the mystery. Having entered it out of love to be one with all humanity, he introduces a new vital energy into it which cannot be suffocated.

And here the Father's plan begins to be manifest. The stark truth of what it means to be human reveals the truth of God. A death so mercilessly human reveals that this dead man is truly the Son of God.

When Jesus, before the Sanhedrin, verbally announces that he is the Son of God, he is rejected. This is not so surprising. It is difficult for man to accept that Jesus is God. It is easier to accept idols. However, when dying on the cross as a poor man he cries out to God, then it is possible to believe that he himself "truly was the Son of God." A human being who while dying calls to God can be the most convincing argument that God exists.

By falling headlong into death Jesus unveils the mystery of it and gives us a glimpse of God who dwells beyond it. In the grip of death which reduces everyone to a state of powerlessness, he sees the only valid solution: to continue loving. This is faithfulness to God to the end through love. Even if God appears absent, Jesus knows that by love's very nature God cannot reject those who abandon themselves to love, because he is love.

Love cannot fail. The Crucified is strong. "He saves himself" and he saves humanity. His cry is not one of despair but of abandonment to love. He is responsible for humanity, both as God and as man. Thus someone will be able to say, "This man truly was the Son of God."

According to Mk, the veil between heaven and earth is torn open three times to proclaim the divinity of Jesus: at his baptism, during the transfiguration, and on Calvary. Here the voice of God does not come thundering down from the sky nor is it proclaimed by an angel, but it is cried out from the agonizing body of the Crucified.

The death of Christ has certainly introduced the possibility of salvation into human death. It is now the threshold where

Jesus awaits each human being. There, those who have never met him or who have always rejected him have one last chance to look into his eyes and to feel his love. A dignified acceptance of human destiny could possibly be the last purification.

*O my Jesus, no one understands me as you do. I must come to you with my problems instead of worrying and running to many mediators. You alone guarantee that all of our experiences are valid. You alone have canceled any reason for despair from human life.*

Jesus' experience on the cross teaches me that I can look for the Crucified not only on Calvary, but also in other places. I can encounter him on all roads and in all homes, wherever a human being is present. I must be ready and able to meet him whenever I encounter another person.

## 3. THE CROSS AND THE DISCIPLE

Mk uses darker tones than Mt to describe the lack of preparation of the disciples for the Passion. They are always in the limelight but they do not always come out shining. They are the closest to Jesus, intimate followers, attentive to his teachings, aiming for celestial rewards. But they are slow to understand, obtuse and narrowminded before the generous perspectives of their teacher.

Following Jesus is difficult. It begins when one freely chooses Jesus. The response, too, is free, but the motivation is confusing. It must be purified and set straight through a conversion process, which involves a continual freeing of oneself from the temptations of power, sluggishness, escape, denial and betrayal.

The lifestyle which Jesus lives and expects others to live does not agree with the disciples. Jesus speaks of giving one's life, of dying for the Gospel, taking up one's cross, of being last and serving all. The disciples discuss who is the greatest among them and continue to wait for the teacher to establish his kingdom on earth.

The idea of the cross does not stick. It is like trying to save a file in a computer which does not have the corresponding software. When the cross appears it results in a deafening collision with shattered ideals. It is like a deadly accident. They cannot understand how this can be possible.

The scattering of the group, Peter's denial and even Judas' despair can be explained not so much as a rejection similar to that of his adversaries, but as the impossibility of recognizing the beloved teacher in the man reduced to such a state. You also were one of his disciples! No. This cannot be the Jesus that I followed and that I even recognized as God.

A God with a cross is out of reach for the human intellect. And faith was still fragile.

In Mk following Jesus also ends happily. The disciples are summoned together and reconstituted by the Risen Lord in Galilee. They are forgiven and purified. The Passion has made them ready to receive the transforming gift of faith. They are no longer the same. They have understood many things that Jesus' community must not forget. Here are the main things:

The cross always catches us by surprise. We can never guarantee that we are ready for it.

Conversion is a process that never ends. There are always false values which stick to us and temptations which do not leave us—they always go against the cross.

Jesus' community must be a humble community, because it has experienced that if it trusts only in itself it will fail time after time. Triumphalism or claim to historical successes in terms of numbers and power is an affront to the cross, whose victory exists uniquely in that love which is life-giving. Being proud of Christ's cross does not mean to wave it like a flag bearer in a parade, but to humbly invoke it like a gift, trying one's best to accept it as an integral part of life, conscious that an unreachable distance separates us from it. Everything which is not love that gives up itself to the end is an insult to the cross of Jesus. The disciple is always far away even though he is always on his journey. Thus he must be capable of reconciliation and of leaving space for the strangers that the cross may attract.

*O my Jesus, help me to understand and live the glory and the humility of the cross. Do not allow the fracture between enthusiasm for the cross and the incapacity to live it occur in me. Help me not to reduce the cross to an ideology but make it life.*

The cross does not mean only pain and death. The most difficult aspect of the cross may be the nonconformity to the world since it is subject to sin. I must follow the Crucified in this permanent tension, not only when I am ill or when I have special problems.

# III. LUKE

## 1. The cross, the revelation of God as Merciful Father

**Reflect.** The ultimate assurance of the Crucified is that he knows and feels that he is the Son. He knows that not even death can separate him from the Father, and thus it is bearable, despite the pain and rejection. Death reveals each human being in his entirety, even Jesus. In death ephemeral values fall away and only what counts remains. We always remember with special fondness the last words or gestures of those dear to us.

Lk demonstrates that throughout his life Jesus placed his relationship with the Father above all others. His mother, his relatives and fellow villagers, his friends, his disciples, the people, his adversaries, his work and his ministry are all bound up with the essential bond with his Father. In the Passion his life is immersed in intimacy with the Father as is demonstrated by the three prayers which articulate his final journey.

In Gethsemane, before being handed over to the darkness, he opens his heart to the Father, disclosing to him the anxiety of his exhausted humanity: "Father, if it is your will, take this cup away from me; nevertheless, not my will but yours be done," 22:42. He wants to be freed, but above all he wants to be faithful to the Father.

Nailed to the cross, and with death closing in upon him, he does not think of himself but of the mission entrusted to him by the Father, to save humanity. With the responsibility of one who is diligently carrying out his task he pleads with the Father: "Father, forgive them for they know not what they are doing," 23:34.

As he is dying, the most revealing of prayers emanates from

his lips and from his heart: "Father, into your hands I commend my spirit," 23:46. God remains Father and Jesus feels that he is Son, even as death separates him from all other relationships. His relationship with the Father is untouchable. In fact, Jesus affirms this with the most expressive gesture possible for a son: he hands himself over to his Father as an ongoing act of love, while all else disappears.

In the conclusion of the Gospel, Lk offers seven arguments to demonstrate that the Father is present and that he responds: a pagan proclaims that Jesus is innocent, a member of the Sanhedrin gives him a burial reserved for a righteous man, the crowds repent, the tomb is found to be empty, Jesus reappears alive, his work continues through the Holy Spirit, he ascends to the right hand of the Father.

The Father's primary quality is love, which Lk expresses as mercy in its most exceptional form. This motif pervades the Gospel, so much so that Lk is called the evangelist of mercy. But in his narrative of the Passion the themes of liberation from evil and forgiveness of sin are accentuated.

To the Passover Supper, which was the remembrance of the Jews' liberation from Egypt, Jesus gives the meaning of our liberation from sin through his imminent death. He ardently desired it. During the transfiguration he had called it his exodus. The bread of his table becomes his body which is shared, and the wine becomes his blood which is poured out. His death is for the forgiveness and transformation of all.

The journey to the cross proclaims the same message. Jesus prays that the attack by Satan will not destroy the faith of Peter and the disciples. He reattaches the ear of one who is an enemy. He draws Peter back to him with a glance of love. He forgives those who crucify him and takes a partner in crucifixion to paradise with him. At his death a pagan is illuminated by faith, the people ask for forgiveness, the disciples do not scatter even if they waver, a member of the Sanhedrin comes forward to claim his body. "The conversion and forgiveness of sins" that Jesus' community must preach always and everywhere is already in motion.

**Pray.** *O my Jesus, nothing can ever be greater than the love that the Father expressed through you. No rejection can ever expel or annul it.*

**Promise.** I must consider my life in the context of God's merciful love, not in the light of my own qualities or energies. God always loves me, even if I don't realize it or reject it. As long as I am alive it is possible to come in contact with his love. I must not cause it to fail. To do so would be life's ultimate failure.

## 2. LOVE OVERCOMES SIN AND DEATH

Jesus did not experience sin but was destroyed by the consequences of sin. Satan did not succeed in bending him to idolatry, as he succeeds with other human beings, but he certainly tried to destroy him with the consequences of sin, which Jesus shouldered and shared with us.

From the beginning of the Passion, Lk notes that "Satan entered into Judas," 22:3. According to the Old Testament pain and death are the consequences of sin. They are the instruments with which the devil destroys humanity. He kills us all. No one can escape. He planned to eliminate Jesus as he does everyone else. Jesus is a man, a "son of Adam"; thus he will leave the scene as all people do, despite his prayer to be liberated.

Pain and death, the destructive consequences of sin, assail him, press in on him from every side and crush him. A disciple betrays him, another denies him, the rest distance themselves from him. The leaders reject him and hate him. Herod makes a mockery of him and Pilate does not take his side because he is afraid of losing his power. No one defends him and no one loves him. Any form of support, understanding, respect and human relationship is severed. Only insults and derision remain, signs of rejection.

No part of his humanity and of the good he has accomplished is accepted. Physical pain takes hold of his body and consumes it like a fire: the arrest, the blows, the shoves, the slaps, the spit, the flagellation, the crown of thorns, perhaps the cardiac arrest in Gethsemane, the journey to Calvary carrying the cross, his wrists and feet pierced with nails, the flesh invaded by tetanus which burns like spreading lava.

What can he do in such a state? There is nothing else that he can do. He has been seized by sin without ever being a sinner. He is under Satan's power. He is a breath away from being destroyed and disappearing as happens to all human beings.

Jesus still has something to do, in fact he has yet to accomplish his greatest work: to love. Out of love he freely chose to be there where he is. He does not love sin, but those who are under the power of sin reduced him to such a state. He loves and accepts these people, these wounds and this death, because for him they are signs of love.

In such a manner the signs of hatred and of death lose their oppressive violence.

Who can they flail against? Against a barrier of love? Who should they destroy? A love which the more you want to destroy it the more powerful it becomes?

The vise loosens. Its grip is broken. Sin is conquered. It has nothing else to destroy. It is useless for it to attack love. It always turns out the loser. It is always vanquished. It is as if someone attacks you to destroy you and you welcome him with an embrace and a smile.

By entering the darkness of death Jesus gives himself to the Father for us. He is not swallowed up by Satan who was waiting as usual for his prey. His death is not the consequence of a fatal destiny, but the consequence of his love and his free choice to give his life out of love. This was a fatal error for Satan who thought that he would have been the winner. This is a new way to live death for all of us.

*O my Jesus, you taught me how to make death a positive experience. In my supreme solitude you will always be there. When I will have to abandon everyone and when all will have to abandon me, I hope to be able to make the only valid choice: to trust in you.*

We often miss opportunities, personal and collective, to discover the meaning of the cross. Personal and communal limitations, hardships in our human relationships, our work, our family and community responsibilities, natural disasters, national and international conflicts, all offer opportunities to come closer to the cross. Do I value these situations as reminders of the cross?

### 3. EVIL MUST DISAPPEAR

What happens to the power of evil after the death and resurrection of Jesus?

Lk accentuates, more than the other evangelists, the clash between good and evil in the Passion. Jesus continually warns his disciples about the seriousness of the test. He does not mean to dramatize, but wants them to understand that the final battle with the forces of darkness is taking place. Darkness launches its most powerful weapon, death.

But there is no doubt about the final outcome. Evil is defeated. It unchained its fury on Jesus and exhausted itself. The conclusion of the Gospel affirms that good is now inextinguishable while evil, even as it continues, can be defeated. It is like a wild beast which can still bite, but bears a mortal wound and eventually must die.

Pain and death are opportunities for Satan to turn us away from God. Now they turn against Satan because Christ has transformed them into the possibility of love and thus salvation.

When he experiences death, Jesus takes possession of it and chooses to give himself out of love. Suffering and death, while remaining consequences of sin and thus arms in Satan's arsenal, have been taken from the enemy's battlefield and have become signs of Jesus' free decision to love. Like him, we also can take hold of our suffering and death when it should arrive, and turn it into the greatest act of love. Satan, who takes advantage of such circumstances to play with temptation, realizes that for us they are all opportunities for love.

All temptations take aim at the cross, because from it emanates the energy of divine love. The cross of Christ represents the defeat of Satan and of his temptations.

It is sufficient to analyze the mechanism of the capital sins. They instigate us to reject the cross of love which requires us to be faithful to God, to others and to ourselves. They incite us to flee from God's will which consists in making Christ, who surrenders himself to the cross for us, our example and model. The will of God and love for the cross coincide. Temptation clashes with both.

Jesus' cross is the only solution both to physical suffering and moral evil. Physical pain cannot be eliminated by God because it is not caused by him but is a consequence of sin, freely chosen by human beings. God did much more than eliminate it: he shared it with us and he offered us the ability of transforming it into love.

God cannot eradicate moral evil in human beings for the same reason. Yet God-man accomplished much more. In his confrontation with Satan he defeated evil. He did not fall prey to his temptations, but he rather transformed the ruins of sin into possibilities of love.

By dying on the cross for us, Jesus not only showed us his love, he also revealed the enormity of sin, for to redeem it he chose to die. He gave us an idea of how monstrous it is to reject God's love, since in order to return it to his Father on behalf of us, he consumed himself out of love.

The Crucified reveals to us not only God's boundless love but also our own corrupt nature. As sinners we were incapable of loving as we ought. Through his innocence he is able to express to the Father the love which we have denied him because of sin. Thus he obtains forgiveness for us and gives us his same ability to love.

Sin has been defeated in the sense that it no longer possesses an undisputed power. One day, its absolute defeat will be manifested. It can still harm because Satan is more intelligent than human beings and can deceive them, and because people are free to give him power over them. Besides Satan's astuteness, sin consists in the incorrect use of human freedom. Yet, the forgiveness that comes down from the cross can at any moment snatch Satan's prey away from him. This happens in a special way through the sacrament of reconciliation.

*O my Jesus, evil would disappear from my life if I were to give space to the power of your cross and resurrection. Evil hurts me still because my freedom gives it weapons. Good which is left undone gives strength to evil. Allow this contradiction to be eliminated from my life.*

Satan, with his temptations, is at the center of humanity's history. In the beginning he convinced man that he could be divine without God. On the path to revelation he persuaded God's people to expect the promised land without passing through the desert. Today, he creates the illusion that we can find happiness without the cross. The perennial temptation also faces me. I must unmask and resist it.

### 4. DEATH, THE BEST OF LIFE

There are diverse interpretations on what awaits us after this life: to take wing to freedom or to precipitate into nothingness; to live in gardens of happiness or to bloom again in other forms of life; to enter into the fullness of life in communion with God and with our brothers and sisters.

Jesus' death on the cross brings clarity also to this aspect of life's drama. Lk presents Jesus' ministry and paschal mystery as a journey from Galilee to Jerusalem, from his Passion and death to the house of the Father. The goal is to return home, but to arrive there he must pass through suffering and death. It is part of the journey. It is foreseen and part of the plan. Even if the journey does not end there this is the most important point, thus it must be lived better than all the other stages.

Jesus does not romanticize death, nor does he fall headlong into a pit of depression. He feels overwhelmed by death, as any human being does. It is Satan's last opportunity to sift us like grain. Death is life's enemy because it severs all relationships and throws us into nothingness. Death is ugly no matter how much we try to embellish it. Give to death what belongs to death.

But give to God's power what rightly belongs to God's power. Lk's Jesus shows us that it is possible to pass through death's suffering with the anchor firmly planted in the world beyond, and through love break through to a new and more abundant life.

This is the paschal death.

Can death become life's goal? That would be absurd. Human intelligence rebels against such a thought. This is not what Jesus intends, even if the evangelists accentuate the importance which Jesus attaches to his own death. We cannot make death life's goal. Life's goal is love. For Jesus it is the love of the Father and of humanity which lies beneath the desperate need for salvation.

Death is a crossing over which allows one to reach these objectives of love and to put love, hindered by the barrier of sin, back into circulation. Christ's death is the most powerful propulsion of life from creation onwards. For this reason the Passion and death of Jesus is also the most astonishing provocation that ever took place in history.

Lk describes Jesus' death as if it were a public testimonial of his identity and his mission. He dies a hero's death, in keeping with his Gospel teachings. After his ministry, with all its lessons and miracles, death is the most effective opportunity to witness the new plan of life lived by him and proposed to his disciples.

In today's society Christians are no different than others even in the way they die. Death is witness to nothing, as often is life. One dies in hospitals. We obliterate death from our thoughts and from daily conversations, even if the media reminds us of it persistently. We need to regain possession of death as the culminating point of our life.

We must speak of it and prepare ourselves for it. This is our last deed and we must take heed to do it with care, better than all other business. It would be of no use to us to have done all else well in life, to have achieved success and well-being if we botch up our final and most important task.

*O my Jesus, fear of death is inevitable. Do not allow me to be overwhelmed by it, but help me to overcome it by approaching it with you as my model.*

I must renew my life insurance policy each day by reciting these words: "Holy Mary, Mother of God, pray for us sinners now and at the hour of our death." In whatever moment, manner or place it should occur, my death has already been entrusted to my mother Mary. She will be with me, just as she was with the dying Jesus.

## 5. THE PASSION, PROOF OF DISCIPLESHIP

The Passion of Jesus is also the passion of the disciple. Not only in the sense of mystical identification, but also in a causal or motivating sense. The Passion reveals the disciple's unpreparedness before the cross.

The narratives of the Passion are a catechesis on discipleship. This is especially true for Lk, even though he portrays less violence than his Synoptic colleagues in pointing out the disciples' weakness. Lk warns the community that the Passion will harvest victims, because faithfulness to the Gospel is costly and not all are ready to pay the price. It is necessary to be vigilant at all times. Because of its nature the Gospel and those who announce it will be attacked by evil.

Conscious of the disciples' frailty, Jesus moves ahead with his testimonial of love to the very end. Those who accompany him are not neutral observers, but they represent different types of followers. Jesus' attitudes in the various events of the Passion are laid out like lessons on discipleship—above all his death on the cross.

On the way to Calvary, the Cyrenean is a mature follower, who has understood the responsibility of carrying the cross behind Jesus, while the women of Jerusalem must purify their reasons for following him and clarify their motives.

On the cross, the lesson is given as if from a pulpit and subdivided into points. First, forgiveness is for all, even if they do not ask for it. In whatever moment one becomes open to it, he or she will be made free from the burden of sin.

Second, forgiveness is infallibly given to those who ask for it. The cross can soon grant salvation. It transforms hearts by bringing about conversion and grants forgiveness. Whoever is capable of recognizing that: "We indeed have been condemned justly, for we are receiving the due reward of our deeds, but this man has done nothing wrong," Lk 23:41, is ready to make the leap into the arms of mercy.

The disposition to follow Jesus extends to a "rethinking" of what has happened. The crowds returning from Calvary reflect upon what has happened and are converted. It is possible that Lk is thinking about Jesus' mother, the first and most perfect disciple, presented by him at the beginning of the Gospel as one who "kept all these things, pondering them in her heart," 2:19 and 51.

Perhaps the disciples are not on Calvary, or perhaps they are those whom Lk mentions as "his acquaintances" who stood at a distance. It does not matter. Lk is really making reference to a universal disciple. Every Christian and every man and woman who will read or listen to the Gospel is a learner. It is necessary to understand that pain is not a curse. Human science can continue its efforts to relieve it, but it will be insufficient to eliminate it from the face of the earth.

We must understand that we are not to expect miracles, instead we must make the miracle of faith and of love happen. Faith does not expect God's intervention to free us from problems because the intervention has already occurred: Christ crucified.

The cross seems to be the end of all. For this reason the disciples fell apart, and the same happens to many Christians of all times. To fortify them the accounts of the Passion have been written. They demonstrate that the cross is not the end but the necessary passage for life to burst into its fullness.

*O my Jesus, the weakness of the disciples during the Passion is reason for trepidation and humility. I cannot for any reason consider myself superior to any of them.*

Jesus' disciples must commit themselves to freeing the world from the pollution of sin. We can be justly preoccupied with terrestrial pollution, yet this world will eventually end. There will be new heavens and a new earth. Instead, the human spirit lasts forever. The cross reclaims its supremacy and its salvation. I must concern myself with the values of the spirit in the name of fellowship with Jesus.

# IV. JOHN

## 1. THE CROSS, THE ULTIMATE SIGN

**Reflect.** According to Jn, Jesus reveals the Father in all of his words and gestures. The first two parts of Jn's Gospel consist of signs and speeches. He does not recount many miracles, but only the few he considers necessary to demonstrate that the power and the love of God are at work in the world.

The miracles are: the changing of the water into wine at Cana, the healing of the son of the royal officer in Capernaum and of the paralyzed man by the pool of Bethesda in Jerusalem, the multiplication of the loaves and the walking on the water, the curing of the man born blind, and the resurrection of Lazarus.

The discourses are often intertwined with the signs. With them Jesus explains the meaning of the miracles or responds to the objections of his opponents.

But no sign or speech is as clear and irrefutable as the sign of the Passion. It confirms whatever Jesus said, and crowns it with the seal of a love that exceeds every expectation or imagination. In Jn's Passion narrative the revelation of the divine identity of Jesus marks every passage, both by words and by symbolism.

In Gethsemane he introduces himself as the "I am" which throws his adversaries to the ground.

While being interrogated by the religious authority, he tells the high priest to check out public opinion regarding his image.

Before the Roman authority he reaffirms the "I am" of his identity and tries to instruct the pagan procurator about it. When Pilate presents him to the people, obviously deprived of every shred of his human dignity, he reveals the fullness of what it means to be human. "Behold the Man," assumed by the divine Word to make possible in human terms the expression of God's love. "Behold the Man" culminates in "Behold your King." This is the offer—take it or leave it.

On the cross Jesus reveals the same facets of his divine identity, but displays them from a universal stage rather than from a secluded tribunal. There, Jesus is in the same condition: disfigured as man, to signify that God reveals himself in broken human nakedness. But he is lifted up on high, for all to see and understand. Instead of directly commenting on the scene, Pilate this time dictates a caption and wants it to be written in all the current languages.

In the pangs of death the Crucified declares that he is thirsty, that is, he ardently longs to see God's love overflowing on humanity in the outpouring of the Spirit. When this occurs, he proclaims that "It is finished"—everything has been accomplished. And the ongoing accomplishment continues down through the centuries, flowing from his pierced heart.

Jn's theological and narrative power is able to transform the cross from a somber instrument of death into a sign of superabundant love. Jesus' death is *the* hour of all hours of time. It is Jesus', God's, humanity's, the world's hour, as well as the hour of the defeat of Satan.

We cannot miss perceiving the mysterious atmosphere of triumph that pervades the Passion narrative according to Jn. He describes all the acts of the tragedy, like the other evangelists: arrest, trial, flagellation, ill treatment in the praetorium, death sentence, nailing to the cross and death. Yet the sensation of disaster is missing.

Jesus had always spoken about this as the hour of his glory, of the manifestation of love, of the return to his home, God's dwelling-place of love. Never does he show the demeanor of one who has been defeated—not even for a split second.

The cross itself is the last word, more powerful than the seven words he spoke from it. It is the word of the Word, pronounced in all its fullness. It is of no use to seek or to expect other words or signs from God. Missing this means to miss the last chance ever. Therefore it is necessary to act in memory of it and to keep it always in our hearts.

**Pray.** *O my Jesus, your Passion is the sign of your love and of the love of the entire Blessed Trinity. May it always be in my heart.*

**Promise.** The God revealed by the Crucified is not a God eager to settle the score, a judge who measures according to human estimation. He is not looking to catch us in a fault in order to punish us, but he is waiting for us to be converted in order to show us his infinite love. This is the God of my life. I want to bear witness to his love with all my strength.

## 2. THE CRUCIFIED JUDGES THE WORLD

The subject on trial is not really Jesus but sin, and by sin our responsibility is meant.

In Jn's account Jesus is always in a conflicting rapport with the Jewish authority. Through his words and actions he reveals God's identity and God's plan for humanity, but this can be rejected by human freedom. Rejecting God, however, is like choosing death or darkness or falsehood or unbelief. One cannot settle for half measures. Jn's narrative is characterized by the use of absolute terms, and for this reason his Gospel lends itself to pitiless anti-Semitic interpretation.

The Passion is the final stage of the conflict. It starts with the backsliding of Judas, the only disciple to be swallowed up by the darkness. Peter just skims it.

The contention grows stronger when the opposition of the "Jews"—as Jn calls them with a negative connotation—jells. They barricade themselves beyond any possibility of understanding. They dare even to claim fidelity to Caesar so as to obtain a death sentence against Jesus.

The Passion is facilitated by the cowardice of Pilate. He remains entangled in a web of compromises and misses the opportunity to encounter the Savior face to face. Even though he rebuffs the accusations of the Jews against Jesus and proclaims Jesus' innocence four times, his efforts are not motivated by faith, therefore they fail under the pressure of the enemies. He practically takes position with them, on the side of darkness.

Away from the stage, Satan works hard. He is the hidden conspirator, the prince of darkness, the father of lies who rushes upon Jesus and incites everyone else to pounce upon him. He is the real head of the opposition, and thus the real accused in this trial. The Passion is not only a tragic human mistake. The forces of evil have woven a plot to eliminate Jesus—obviously in the context of his free determination to give up his life.

Jesus dominates the situation even though he may seem caught up in the whirl of the hurricane. His preeminence results not only from his words but also from his attitude and powerful gestures. In the garden of Gethsemane he does not prostrate himself in anguished prayer, but rather he casts the guards down before consenting to his arrest. He had already made his prayer during the Supper, sitting at the table and talking with the Father as equals about the coming events.

During the trials he doesn't show the slightest embarrassment. On the contrary he puts others in an embarrassing position. It does not seem that it is he who is under investigation but the others. Instead of asking ourselves what is going to happen to him we are rather inclined to ask: What will happen to Annas, Caiaphas, Pilate, the members of the Sanhedrin?

He is not silent like the Suffering Servant who remains completely wordless, but he talks, he speaks like the judge who is to come on the clouds of heaven.

He does not die uttering a loud cry, but imparting the last instructions for the future and explaining the meaning of what is happening.

The culmination of the power of darkness—that is of lies, unbelief and death—coincides with the culmination of the Christian message—the death of Jesus out of love to the end.

The two pinnacles meet: the one of wickedness against the one of love. One of them is destined to be defeated. Jesus' death is the victory of God's power, which is love. Jesus' death is also the final judgment over the power of evil, which is defeated at the same time in which it seems to be winning.

Evil does not have the power to destroy love. In fact, the more the forces of evil try to quench Jesus' love, the more they make it emerge and stand out; the more they hurl themselves against him to eliminate him, the more they give him the opportunity to show his love.

This is the verdict of defeat and of condemnation against Satan who always is the head of the forces of evil. By unchaining their fury against Jesus, they led him precisely where he wanted to go: to give up his life out of love, thus revealing and bestowing upon humanity the love of God.

*O my Jesus, nothing indeed can be alien to your cross. Acceptance or rejection, absolution or condemnation are connected with it. It is planted in my life and in the center of creation, vertically and horizontally reaching and conditioning everything.*

The true judgment on human life is not pronounced by tribunals but by the cross of Christ. It is the cross that determines our successes and failures. It declares whether our choices and behavior before the problems of history such as progress, rationalism, consumerism, social injustice, etc. are right or wrong. I must be concerned about what the cross of Christ says about me, not about what others say.

## 3. THE CROSS, AN INDISPUTABLE ARGUMENT

The topic is love. It was necessary to develop the theme in a way that cannot be contested by human intelligence. The human mind questions everything and objects about everything, even God. It is not easy to convince the reasoning being! God, who thus created him, accepts the challenge to confront him.

To die on the cross out of love is such a breathtaking argument that it leaves the human being speechless.

By becoming human, the Word of God becomes an expert in humanity and understands how to make himself understood. He found the way to convey divine truths to the receptacle of the human brain. Among these there is the cross. Now here there is nothing to object to. A God who does not consider it unbecoming to serve men, to wash their feet, even to die on the cross for them, can be understood by everyone. One can reject him, but one cannot avoid taking him into consideration.

The state of religious life in the Church finds its theological foundation in the *kenosis* of the divine Word, that is in Jesus Christ emptying himself of his own divinity in the incarnation. Religious vows are the highest way of expressing in human terms the love that is within the Blessed Trinity and has been communicated to us. This powerful discourse on God reaches its summit on the cross.

Jn develops this topic through symbols spread along the entire Passion narrative, but adds another symbol beyond death: the pierced heart. It is the symbol of a love that breaks down every barrier.

The subject is similar to that of mercy in Lk's Gospel, but the language in Jn contains a special symbolic effectiveness.

Jesus had affirmed that he was going to manifest his love for his disciples to the end, but the word "end" cannot mean that his love comes to an end like all human things and values. Rather it means that Jesus loves them to the ultimate expression of love. This cannot even be the cross, which would be the end for a human being, but not for God. Therefore the open heart manifests a love beyond love, the divine love that is still being poured out beyond the maximum that man can perceive.

God's love is infinite, because it is God himself. The cross knocks down the wall of the finitude of human love and plugs it into the circuit of divine love, which is infinite. There, beyond love, there is always love.

This theological synthesis has been brilliantly described by one of the Fathers of the Church, probably St. Augustine, in this way: "Though he is the Almighty, he was unable to do more. Though he is the Omniscient, he was unable to invent something wiser. Though he is the richest, he had nothing more to give." He could not, knew not, had nothing more. In love he exhausted the possible. Not by reason of his own powerlessness, but because the recipient—humanity—cannot contain more. Love overflows everywhere.

By recounting the incident of the pierced heart, Jn is aware that he is transmitting an extraordinary revelation. Jesus is dead, but he is not finished. Now the most important scene is coming. We must look at the one who has been transfixed, keep our eyes on him always, for love and life arise from him forever.

The mystery of the Crucified means not only that he died for us, but also that this love flows upon us and renders us able to love to that same point. The open and bleeding heart of Jesus is the sign of the overflowing of love that is the effusion of the Holy Spirit.

The preface of the feast of the Sacred Heart thus celebrates this love: "Lifted high on the cross, Christ gave his life for us, so much did he love us. From his wounded side flowed blood and water, the foundation of sacramental life in the Church. To his open heart the Savior invites all to draw water in joy from the springs of salvation."

*O my Jesus, your love is convincing indeed! Awestruck before it, there is nothing more I can do but believe, adore, give thanks and accept it with all my heart.*

In response to the love of the Crucified, I resolve to confirm and to increase my commitment to relieve the painful situation of those who are near to me in this time of history. My meditation on the Crucified would be of no use if I am not able to recognize Jesus in the crucified people of humanity.

## 4. THE CRUCIFIED, AN IRRESISTIBLE ATTRACTION

One of the terms with which Jesus hints at his death is "exaltation." Other words also used are: the giving up of life, his hour, to be handed over, return to his Father. However "exaltation" or "lifting up" is probably the most puzzling expression to indicate his death on the cross. From the simple and degrading gesture of planting a cross on the ground with a human body hanging on it, there is the switch to the idea of elevation and re-entry into the glory of the Trinity.

While the Synoptics mark Jesus' journey to Jerusalem with three predictions of his coming Passion, Jn interposes among the signs and discourses of Jesus three allusions to his exaltation on the cross.

The first is found in the nocturnal dialogue with Nicodemus. "As Moses lifted up the serpent in the wilderness, so must the Son of Man be lifted up, that whoever believes in him may have eternal life," Jn 3:14.

The second takes place at the hottest point of a controversy with the Jews, who accused him of not giving sufficient credentials about himself. "When you have lifted up the Son of Man, then you will know that I am he, and that I do nothing on my own authority but speak thus as the Father taught me," Jn 8:28.

The third time happens after a voice from heaven assured that Jesus would be glorified. "When I am lifted up from the earth, I will draw all men to myself," Jn 12:35.

The full disclosure of Jesus' power of attraction is conditioned to his elevation on the cross, not to his resurrection as we would expect. Both moments constitute the same reality, but if resurrection were to be considered separately, it could appear a showing off of divine power and could make us feel estranged.

Jn concludes his Passion narrative quoting the prophet Zechariah 12:10: "They shall look on him whom they have pierced," 19:37, as if to say that humanity's eyes should be permanently turned toward the Crucified. In the troubled human comedy no scene is worthier. It contains everything.

Resurrection is ready to explode, like the big-bang of the new creation. Jesus' death is like a pregnant womb, from which resurrection is going to be born. Resurrection can be compared to a detonator set off by the Crucified in the very center of history. Everything is destined to be transformed by the Risen Lord.

The Crucified is like the reservoir of all the positive possibilities embodied in God, in humanity and in creation. He is the highest point of revelation of all God's mysteries and plans: God Trinity, God Love, creation, incarnation, the outpouring of the Holy Spirit, the sense and destination of humanity. He reveals all about God and about the human being: how great God is and how much he can lower himself; how mean the human being is and to what point he can be lifted up. He is the law of gravity that keeps all things together.

Vatican II reminded us that the Word of God, by becoming incarnate, united himself "in a certain way" to every human being (*Pastoral Constitution on the Church in the Modern World*, n. 22). Thus, being elevated on the cross he attracts to himself in a certain way every human being, and in his resurrection he brings with himself in a certain way all the men and women of the world.

Jesus' paschal mystery, and the newness of life he granted to us, so intimately pervades the innermost tissues of humanity that it makes humanity able to realize at least partially in history the primordial plan of God—even though with fatigue, only gradually and "in a certain way." The allurement of sin reaps many victims still, but no one can completely ignore the attraction of the Crucified.

*O my Jesus, may I feel the attraction of your crucified love in a more resolute manner. Help me to contemplate your presence and to meet you when I attend to my brothers and sisters.*

The crucified Lord is the strongest reason for confidence we can find in human history. From him we draw energy when we succeed and forgiveness when we fail. I commit myself to be a witness to this truth in a special way, through my Christian behavior.

## 5. HIS WOUNDS DAZZLING WITH LIGHT

Jesus physically died because of the many wounds in his body. Not only those caused by the nails in his hands and feet but also those inflicted by the flagellation and other abusive treatments.

Jn suggests that the wounds are also the cause for Jesus' resurrection, since they are the signs of his love. No one else like Jn gives so much importance to the wounds of the Risen Lord. The paschal faith of the disciples depends on the fact that they recognized Jesus from his wounds. "He showed them his hands and his side. Then the disciples rejoiced when they saw the Lord," Jn 20:20.

Even Thomas, the most unbelieving and rationalist among them, surrenders and makes room for faith before the dazzling truth of the wounds. "Bring your finger here and look at my hands; and put out your hand and place it in my side; be not unbelieving, but believe," Jn 20:27.

Most probably Thomas did not need this materialistic test, but the association between faith and the wounds of the Risen Lord is by now established for all believers. Jesus would not allow the loving Mary Magdalene to touch him. By entering into the new relationship with the Resurrected she will understand that the bond of faith is totally different from the one of hugs and kisses. But when required, Jesus offers even the physical guarantee of his wounds.

They are now not only wounds but glorious wounds, because they are proof of both death and resurrection. This is one of the most fascinating themes of Jn's Gospel. While anticipating during the Passion the contents of the resurrection, he then carries into the resurrection the contents of the Passion. The wounds are glorious not only because Jesus is risen, but also because he died out of love, and thus he won out over Satan and sin.

Meditating upon the Crucified and the Risen Lord according to Jn, we are to pay close attention to the wounds. They certify that the one who is risen is the same as the one who died, and explain the link between death and resurrection.

Becoming man, suffering and dying was not something of secondary importance for the Son of God, as if he had taken flesh in order to accomplish the work of salvation and then he got rid of it to return to the state of heavenly glory that he had dismissed in the incarnation. The Word never ceased being in the Blessed Trinity. Now he will never cease belonging to humanity. He goes back to the Father in his glorified humanity, which retains the wounds.

We would expect that Jesus, rising from the dead, would heal his wounds. But he chose not to, in order to express in a symbolic way the power of his love and the resulting glory.

The new life of the Risen Lord cannot even be imagined by our mind. The resurrection is still part of the plan of the incarnation, as the completion of it. The resurrection occurs in history, thus it is a historical event; but at the same time it is also a metahistorical event, since it is operated by God who lives beyond history.

Jesus' humanity rose from the dead and ascended into heaven retaining its wounds. Presenting them to his Father, Jesus shows him how much he loved humanity in his name and intercedes forever in favor of all of us.

The glorious wounds do not emit blood and pain anymore, but only glory and love. What was excruciating Passion on this earth became refulgent glory in heaven.

The wounds of love now shining in heaven act as a counterbalance to the wounds of sin here on earth. Those who feel wounded by pain and defeated by death are invited to contemplate in Jesus what is the final lot of every human suffering if transformed into love.

Those who are the cause of the wounds of their brothers and sisters receive from Jesus' wounds a sentence of condemnation for their wrongdoing. While the wounds that are accepted receive value from love, the wounds that are inflicted can be canceled only by forgiveness.

The wounds of the Crucified call for conversion, disperse salvation and judge history.

*O Jesus, may the light of your wounds enlighten every dark moment or situation in my life and in the life of all humanity.*

There are moments in personal or communal life in which everything seems to be lost. I myself experience it when I am suffering from illness, in solitude or misunderstanding, or when I cannot obtain what I would like. The most positive solution in these incidents would be to transform such an amount of sorrow into love. It is possible. Jesus' wounds guarantee it.

## 6. THE WOMEN WHO STOOD BY THE CRUCIFIED

From a human point of view the cross is the denial of all promises and expectations. From God's perspective however it is the full accomplishment of them. This explains the collapse of faith of the disciples during the Passion.

Only the faith of Mary the mother of Jesus withstands all the contradictions of the facts. It is she, the first believer of the New Testament, who by the cross represents the Church already alive and faithful to her Master. In her faith the Church survives during the dark passage from the Jesus of Nazareth to the paschal Jesus.

All the evangelists remark that the women are more exemplary than the men in following Jesus in the Passion. With this detail the Gospels intentionally convey something meaningful for us, since it comes from a biblical background substantially anti-feminist and from a contemporary culture that is still highly chauvinistic.

At the supper in Bethany, from where the Passion starts, only a woman has the right intuition about Jesus' fate and enters into communion with him. Whoever she might be, she represents the feminine ability to understand others when touched by the cross.

When Peter tries to follow Jesus from afar, one or two women servants of the high priest catch him off guard and make his inconsistency evident.

In the intricate weave of the trial there is one woman only, and even away from the scene, who seriously pays attention to Jesus and asserts his innocence. It is the pagan wife of Pilate, whom some apocryphal writers call Claudia Procla.

On the way to Calvary, Lk imagines that a great multitude follow Jesus, but among them a group of women stand out "who bewailed and lamented him," 23:27. Their solidarity is praiseworthy even though Jesus points out different motivations for their grief.

The presence of the women is brought to our attention in a special way by the cross, where the absence of the disciples is striking. The authors refer to this with an almost pedantic precision, apparently with no reason.

In attendance were "Mary Magdalene, and Mary the mother of James the younger and Joses, and Salome," Mk 15:40-41. "Mary Magdalene, and Mary the mother of James and Joseph, and the mother of the sons of Zebedee," Mt 27:56. "The women who had followed him from Galilee," with no names, Lk 23:49. "Standing by the cross of Jesus were his mother and his mother's sister, Mary the wife of Clopas and Mary Magdalene," Jn 19:25.

We omit inquiring about the list, but it is clear that the intention is to stress the constant presence of the women near the Crucified. The same group will be present at his burial, ready to help and watching the procedure, with Joanna added by Lk, 24:10.

They are the first to see the empty tomb and the first to meet the heavenly messengers announcing the resurrection on Easter morning. The apostles think that the women have been hallucinating. However no one can deny that these women remain at the roots of the Christian faith in the resurrection of Jesus.

Among them Mary Magdalene stands out. It is not easy to retrace her identity, but there is no doubt that her mission is to be the first to announce that the Lord is risen, even to the apostles. While Mary the mother of Jesus cherishes in silence the certitude of faith, Mary Magdalene proclaims and shares the gift of the apparition.

It ensues that there must be a special accord between the women, or the feminine aspect of the human being, and the newness of life generated by the Crucified. This is why their special presence near Jesus is "Gospel," in spite of the fact that their testimony was not relevant under Jewish law.

*O my Jesus, help me to be engaged in witnessing your resurrection with the same commitment and enthusiasm that the women showed after seeing the empty tomb. Grant that my life be a manifestation of your resurrection.*

In the Passion of Jesus the women gave a better example than the disciples. It is not the case to undermine it saying that women did not run risks since their presence was socially irrelevant. They are simply more sensitive to the sorrows of others and more open to communion. And this is a gift for the entire human community.

*May the passion of Jesus*
*And the sorrows of Mary*
*Be always in our hearts!*

# ESSENTIAL BIBLIOGRAPHY

Brown, Raymond E., *La Passione nei Vangeli*, Brescia: Queriniana, 1988.

_____, *The Death of the Messiah, From Gethsemane to the Grave. A Commentary on the Passion Narratives in the Four Gospels.* Two volumes. New York/London/Toronto: Doubleday, 1994.

De la Potterie, Ignace, *The Hour of Jesus.* New York: Alba House, 1990.

_____, *La Passione secondo il quarto evangelista*, Parola per l'Assemblea festiva 19, 41-54, Brescia, Morcelliana.

_____, *La Passione di Gesù secondo il vangelo di Giovanni*, Edizioni Paoline, 1988.

Di Mascio Lorenzoni, A.L., *La crocifissione di Gesù. Un profilo psicologico.* Milano: Ancora, 1989.

Galot, J., *La "Beata Passio,"* Milano: Vita e Pensiero, 1969.

Madott, B.C., *Follow Me: Meditations on the Passion.* Ottawa: Novalis, 1994.

Maggioni, B., *I racconti evangelici della Passione.* Assisi: Cittadella, 1994.

Manaranche, A., *Un amore chiamato Gesù.* Edizioni Paoline, 1990.

Martini, C.M., *I racconti della Passione: Meditazioni.* Brescia: Morcelliana, 1994.

Messori, V., *Patì sotto Ponzio Pilato? Un'indagine sulla Passione e morte di Gesù*, Torino: SEI, 1992.

Pelikan, J., *Jesus through the Centuries. His Place in the History of Culture.* New York: Harper & Row, 1987.

Ravasi, G., *I Vangeli di Pasqua*, Libri di Famiglia Cristiana, 1993.

Rowan, S.C., *Words from the Cross*. Mystic, CT: Twenty-Third Publications, 1988.

Senior, Donald, C.P., *The Passion of Jesus in the Gospel of Mark*. Wilmington, DE: Michael Glazier, 1984.

_____, *The Passion of Jesus in the Gospel of Matthew*. Wilmington, DE: Michael Glazier, 1985.

_____, *The Passion of Jesus in the Gospel of Luke*. Wilmington, DE: Michael Glazier, 1989.

_____, *The Passion of Jesus in the Gospel of John*. Wilmington, DE: Michael Glazier, 1991.

_____, *Jesus, A Gospel Portrait*. New and revised edition. New York: Paulist Press, 1992.

Vanhoye, A., *I racconti della Passione nei vangeli sinottici*. Parola per l'Assemblea festiva 16, 71-124, Brescia: Morcelliana.

Vanhoye, A., De la Potterie, I., Duquoc, Ch., Charpentier, E., *La Passione secondo i quattro vangeli*, UTS, Brescia: Queriniana, 1983.